MAGICAL TALES
The Story-Telling Tradition

12⁹⁵

MAGICAL TALES

The Story-Telling Tradition

R.J. Stewart

Manufactured in the United States of America
ISBN: 1-892137-02-X

Mercury Publishing Inc.
PO Box 493
Lake Toxaway, NC 28747
(828) 884-8783, (828) 884-4875 fax
Web site: www.mercurypublishing.com

Preface to 1998 edition

I am delighted to introduce this 1998 edition of *Magical Tales*, to what I hope will be a new and wider readership. This collection of my short stories was first published in Britain in 1990, and due to the mysterious convoluted processes of the conglomerate publishing industry is still largely unknown in other countries, especially in the USA where it has often been in demand, but rarely supplied. However, this edition, by Mercury Publishing, is intended to remedy the situation. I have also included in this new edition two further episodes from my story cycle *The Woman of the Birds*, which were not in the original edition, but were published separately in *Voices from the Circle* (Aquarian Press 1990) edited by Caitlin Matthews and Prudence Jones.

Since 1990 I have often performed recited or read these stories at workshops, conferences, and gatherings, both with and without music. I feel that stories and songs can and do preserve and communicate levels of awareness that are more then mere words or music: in an age when fable, myth, and potent imagery, have been hijacked by the advertising industry, there is still a place for magical tales. For me that place is in the heart as well as in the head, and though there is an Introduction all about origins and futures of story telling, I recommend that you ignore it until you have the read the stories themselves.

R J Stewart

Inverness, California, 1998

R J STEWART

R J Stewart is a Scot, an author and composer, now living in California. His books have been published in many languages, and he is widely acknowledged as an authority on mythology, legends, magical arts, and ancient traditions. He has also composed and recorded music and songs for feature films, television, and theater productions. His best selling books include *The Merlin Tarot*, *Celtic Gods Celtic Goddesses*, and *The UnderWorld Initiation.* For more information on books, recordings, and workshops and seminars in the USA, see the Stewart web-site at *http://www.dreampower.com*

ACKNOWLEDGEMENTS

I would like to acknowledge those who listened to readings of some of these stories at various Merlin Conferences, gatherings at Hawkwood College, and late at night (the hallowed time for magical tales) in various private locations. Special thanks must be given to Stuart Littlejohn who illustrated the book.

CONTENTS

FOREWORD

The 15 stories in this collection are drawn from among those that I have written over the last 10 years. Several of them are integral parts of long story-cycles (some still opening out) involving a series of interrelated tales, while others come from the unpublished novels *The Woman of The Birds* and *The Fairy Harp*.

Some of these tales arose while I was developing *The Merlin Tarot* and may be highlighted or interpreted by applying images from that deck to the narrative sequence and the main characters. Unlike other short stories which I have published in various anthologies or thematic books, such as *Warriors of Arthur* and *Legendary Britain* (with John Matthews), these are all specifically *magical* tales. Exactly what is implied by the term 'magical tale' is explored in the pages that follow, but like magical tales worldwide these stories are humorous, unsparing, and often disturbing.

If the reader wants warm reassuring escapades full of good magicians and glowing spiritual presences, in which negative forces or frightening beings are banished far away to create a fantasy realm of utmost pleasure and perfection, read no further. If, on the other hand, you wish to find an alternative way into the realms of imaginative or magical transformation, a way which bypasses lengthy textbooks and intellectual analyses (of which I myself stand guilty, among many others), then read on.

There is no claim that this collection of tales, or the introductory essay on story-telling and mythic or poetic traditions, is in any way academically definitive or complete. Why we have such an obsession with completeness, which is often a synonym for rigidity and dogma, has always puzzled me. The great magical mystical poetic and mythic traditions world-wide are never, but never, complete. They are full of open doorways, side-alleys, barely perceived reflections, hints, echoes, even down-right confusing contradictions. One of the powers of magical story-telling is that it explores some of these side-alleys where a religion, a school of metaphysics, or a magical textbook cannot, by its very nature, pass.

Magical and mythic tales from early cultures, and as perpetu-ated in living folk tradition, are often earthy, using vivid language and frank imagery. Due to certain collective problems which we modern people have, only too evident in our popular entertainment, our unfortunate heritage of centuries of repres-sion due to religious-sexual propaganda, such pagan frankness is often misunderstood or misrepresented as gratuitous vulgar-ity. This aspect of the story-telling tradition, therefore, does not appear in its full stature in these stories.

Some of the tales are out of fantastical alternative mythologies and worlds, while others are expansions upon firmly established traditional sources. Having worked for some years with Celtic tradition, I have not hesitated to use certain of the foundational elements of Scottish, Irish, Welsh, or British lore. But I have never indulged in Celtic twilight: there are no Celtic language words inserted like lumps into the text, no posturing Celticisms; I leave such nonsense to others.

Perhaps I am being unfair. Being a Scot with a Welsh mother, I can afford to let my ancestors speak through me in the language of my day, by which I mean not only whatever tongue is con-veniently spoken, but the inter-cultural language which opens out and develops with our dramatic annual increase of world communications. Most of the time, of course, the ancestors remain silent and leave me to write the stories, they being great believers in individual unaided effort and sturdy self-reliance.

R.J. Stewart
Bath, 1989
Inverness, CA, 1998

HOW TO USE
THIS BOOK

Magical tales work directly upon the imagination; they have the potential to bypass our sophistications and our protective shell of habits and touch upon inner sources of transformation, upon spiritual insights. They are also, and this is most important, humorous and disturbing, sometimes simultaneously within one tale. They work through involvement and entertainment in the true sense of the words, wherein we are drawn into a situation and in turn take it into ourselves. In other words, there is an exchange of energies at work.

Due to their connection to enduring traditions of story-telling which embody powerful images and primal narratives shared by humankind world-wide, magical tales can, under certain conditions, attune the individual or group to deep well-springs of imagery and energy. Modern psychotherapy recognizes this connection as a means of tapping into the individual unconscious or collective unconscious mind; the method and its potent results, however, were long established and maintained before any modern psychological framework was devised. Esoteric traditions have a detailed and effective psychology of their own, which may be traced historically to the cultures of Ancient Greece or Egypt, but of course they have a far longer (unproven) life history in terms of human endeavour towards understanding. But magical tales cut through both types of psychology, materialist and esoteric, for they are generated directly out of the master images of our awareness. Details vary, as we might expect, according to culture, geography, language, and historical period, but magical tales world-wide all hold certain key images and narratives in common.

I would recommend that the reader goes straight to the collection of original magical tales in this book, initially without reading their individual introductions, which can be added at a second reading. There is a general expansion or development in the order of the tales; they start with fairly direct and simple stories, gradually becoming more complex. The complexity is not one of style or intellectual content, but of embedded reflections and cross-references. A number of themes stated simply in the earlier tales reappear as foundations or points for departure in later stories. This is exactly how magical traditions work, with a set of basic emblems or patterns which manifest and operate in increasingly complex or paradoxical ways. Fortunately the story-telling tradition is frequently humorous, and even the most serious and apparently difficult concepts are likely to be presented as jests.

Some of the key themes which underpin this collection are common to oral magical tales world-wide, and are central to many magical, meditational or spiritual disciplines. They include, but are by no means limited to:

1. Alternative mythology and legends which parallel those generally known but do not appear in our historical world. These include so called 'heretical' traditions which have been discarded by the world's orthodox religions for political or suppressive reasons. Such traditions are frequently represented by mysterious books or, as we might expect, story-cycles.

2. The ludicrous adventures of a young man or woman, though often the character is male. Traditionally women act as catalysts for either his folly or his education. No sensitivities are spared in the adventures of this youth.

3. Alternative worlds and dimensions which have a potent impact upon our own. These include the traditional world of Fairy, often associated with the primal Underworld[1] of the Ancestors and oldest gods and goddesses, into which mortals physically disappear and from which they may, perhaps, return; and imaginative or mythic locations, which often have a grotesque ambience. Further worlds may contain eternal places, such as primal landscapes, temples, and spiritual cities,[2] while yet others appear to be complete worlds or cultures with historical patterns in their own right.

4. Key characters who appear and reappear in various guises. These are similar to the archetypes posited by modern psychology, but are by no means identical to them, and should not

be confused with them. Some of these characters are found in tarot cards, a set of emblems based upon story-telling traditions and made into picture cards in Renaissance Italy. The traditional characters, however, may be traced back to much earlier periods, and are found in a number of direct literary references and descriptions from as early as the twelfth century. [3]

For those who wish to dissect the matter further, and who have an interest in story-telling traditions and their link to magical or spiritual disciplines and arts, the Introduction to this book ranges through some of the important topics, such as oral tradition, images, visualization, memory, ancient Mysteries, tarot, symbols, and transformative or empowering techniques which are found within traditional and modern magical tales. It also deals with the essential but little understood differences between true magical tales and fiction that uses magical themes for special effect. None of this introductory intellectual discussion is essential to the tales themselves. They are designed to work directly within the imagination, tapping into primal images, other worlds, magical personae, and enduring inner traditions which are, alas, often obscured through intensive detailed esoteric or magical literature in which technicalities tend to mask or even replace actual experience.

Each tale has an individual introduction, and these do not follow a strict pattern. Some offer keys to the more obscure aspects of the tale, or to specific but little-known magical traditions embedded within the tale, while others are merely brief notes on the writing or origin and how it relates to the present collection or to tale-telling traditions in general. Some of the introductions delve into the relationship between magical tales and magical songs, or story-telling and the tarot; such matters are best served in the context of each story, rather than making lengthy factual and theoretical chapters in their own right. Readers who wish to pursue the more detailed esoteric aspects of legend, tarot, magical arts and the like, will find a Bibliography at the end of the book, supported by a few specific notes in this Foreword, the main Introduction and the short introductions to each tale.

The impact of magical tales is at its strongest when the words are read aloud, though this is not a rigid rule and obviously most people will read the stories silently to themselves. It is worthwhile, however, to gather with a like-minded group and take it in turns to read the stories aloud. This applies equally of course to traditional fairy-tales, legends, myths and other magical narratives, all of which were originally part of an oral tradition, in which people gathered together to tell or hear tales, narrative ballads, or epic sagas which combined song and story.

For those who have read the stories and wish to hear them told aloud, or to work with visualization, meditation, and inner transformation commencing from tapes, a set of cassettes of *Magical Tales*, read by the author, is available from Sulis Music, BCM 3721 London WC1N 3XX, as is a cassette of *Magical Songs*, some of which are featured within or as the sources of tales in this collection.

INTRODUCTION

THE ORIGINS AND TRADITIONS
OF MAGICAL TALES

One of the most enduring and important magical traditions is that of story-telling, yet it is the least represented in the twentieth-century revival of occult or esoteric arts and disciplines, possibly because it is the least understood. Magical story telling derives from extremely ancient primal spiritual arts, which originally expressed human understanding of the Creation of the Worlds. More simply, we might say that magical tales are a collective human echo of the story of all Being; certain sacred story-cycles and epics deriving from this primal story were active in Western culture until very recently, while in the East and in many remote areas of the planet such traditions still flourish.

Due to a vast flood of fantasy entertainment in both books and media, modern materialistic cultures increasingly regard story-telling as 'mere fiction'; even the most remote human societies now have access to radio and television, and literacy or the lack of it are no longer relevant as factors in cultural transformation. Thus what was once a magical and sacred matter of tradition, is now easily supplanted and trivialized. It is worth emphasizing that this trivialization is as negative and as effective for the sophisticated individual in a highly material or mechanized society as it is for the primal or isolated tribe.

The weaving of tales was of major importance to our ancestors, not merely for education or the preservation of information, important as these were, but for deep magical transformation. It is upon this level that we may reappraise the story-telling traditions for modern inner development, for this branch of magical art is long overdue for an empowered revival.

We do not have to retreat into a cosy romantic pseudo past, or even into a real but distant historical past, to find magical story-telling traditions. Such traditions are still active in relatively isolated areas of Europe, and are maintained by the native peoples of America and Australasia. In Western societies we find that there are well-documented examples of magical story-cycles and heroic epics from Celtic culture . . . not only in medieval literature (though this preserved many important tales) but also in the twentieth century. Modern traditions of extended story-telling and mythical narratives are well-known from a few European countries, such as Scotland, Ireland, Finland, and some Scandinavian and Mediterranean regions. As such Western examples are directly relevant to our theme, we shall use some of them as our main source of initial discussion before moving deeper into the magical creative process itself, but it should be kept in mind that they have many active unbroken traditional Eastern parallels which are not touched upon.

Before proceeding we must emphasize that *traditional* magical stories and story or epic cycles are not connected in any way with modern fantasy or 'magical' fiction. Even when a writer has consciously borrowed motifs and symbols from genuine traditions, this does not guarantee that the resulting work will inevitably tap into magical or transformative levels of the original tradition. It is this area, the regeneration of primal story-telling as an effective inner agency of transformation, that we shall concentrate upon in our working theory and examples.

MAGICAL TALES DEFINED

What, then, is a *magical tale*? How does it differ from any inspired or contrived fantasy story? To this difficult, but not impossible question we might add: what role, if any, can magical story-telling play in modern materialistic culture, as it did in the past and as it still does in remote regions and societies? The first question can be answered in fairly precise terms, but the second question may only be truly answered through experience, no matter what theory, methods of practice, or examples may be offered upon a printed page or in an explanatory book of this sort.

Magical tales originally emerged from, and were preserved

within, oral traditions. This does not imply that such tales were never written down, for a large number of them were recorded, often as they were passing out of widespread circulation. Arthurian literature of the Middle Ages is a typical example of such a recording and expansion of oral tradition, though we may easily lose sight of the original matter in its complex literary developments.[4] The mythical and heroic sagas of Ireland are another example, and these were still being told in communal situations many centuries after monastic chroniclers first set them out in writing. It seems likely, with Irish and Scottish oral traditions, that the tales were mainly preserved intact through memory alone; in other words they were not drawn from any of the now well-known and translated monastic sources, for these lay untranslated and forgotten until as late as the nineteenth century.[5]

Wales produced a remarkable story-cycle, much of which seems to have been lost, known as *The Mabinogion*, a term which broadly means 'youthful adventures'. This magical and spiritual theme of youthful adventures is vitally important world-wide, and we shall return to it later in our collection of original magical tales.[6]

Thus we may define a magical story as being *embedded within a tradition*. This is an important rule, if accepted, for it immediately disposes of the bulk of modern fiction and fantasy, including many works claiming to be magical. Curiously, it does not dispose of all such matter, and can include many odd items such as certain vastly popular comic books that seem to preserve, albeit unconsciously, some of the old story-telling traditions.[7]

Enduring magical tales, those that were part of long organic collective traditions of story-telling and preservation, were carefully formalized and stylized exercises of the imagination. They were assembled within strict yet flexible boundaries, and held material for men, women, and children of all ages. Certain cycles or types of tale seem to have had special group functions, as we know from comparative anthropology, but this aspect of story-telling is not directly relevant to our main theme, which is one of imagination and awareness rather than social development or custom. Furthermore, many of the reductionist conclusions of anthropology and psychology in connection with traditional lore world-wide may be open to criticism. What may seem to be sexual or peer group roles, dramas, stories and the like to a city based psychologically trained university student, may form part of much wider organic magical and spiritual traditions; the forest is thus ignored while categorizing individual clumps of trees.

MAGICAL TALES, VISUALIZATION, AND THERAPY

One hallmark of magical tales is that they frequently involve familiar characters, often in varied guises; stylized and ritualized adventures; and a repetition that never palled upon the listener. We should always remember that they were recited aloud, with a teller performing to an assembled group. This is of key importance in the magical, transformative function of story-telling, and has direct relevance to magical or spiritual disciplines, which frequently employ set groups of symbols and images in varied combinations, such as the Tree of Life, the Tarot, the Communion of Saints, and so forth. The familiarity and repetition of such units is not, paradoxically, boring and trivial, but leads to deep changes of consciousness in which the units or images, characters or symbols, reveal increasingly powerful harmonics of meaning and energy.[8] We shall return to this important subject again.

In modern arts of visualization or meditation and magical disciplines, *guided imagery* (sometimes incorrectly labelled 'Pathworking') plays a significant role. Such esoteric visualization, in which the vital energies of the individual or group are directed through specific images and sequences, has been undertaken for thousands of years by priests, priestesses and magicians. It is part of a series of well-defined and long established artistic disciplines, held in common by formal religions and magical traditions world-wide, each tradition expressing the art through its regional or national forms. Visualization has recently been 'discovered' as a therapeutic exercise by psychologists, and this use of guided imagery, and indeed of freely generated story-telling, tends to mislead us into assuming that ancient traditions were similar in some way to our modern use. This is not the case.

The two extremes defined, that of inner discipline in visualization and creative imagery, and that of interactive but reductive mental therapy, are opposite or complementary poles in our intentional application of the potent forces of human imagination. Both draw upon an innate property of consciousness . . .

that innermost creative act, a power which remains a mystery no matter what traditional or materialist claims are made to explain it.

UNIQUE ASPECTS OF THE STORY-TELLING TRADITION

Magical story-telling is closer to the disciplines of the great magical or religious traditions than it is to any psychotherapeutic exercise, yet it does not partake fully of either function while fulfilling the purposes of both. It has several levels of potential action: it may be therapeutic or simply educational and reassuring to the listeners, while being highly empowered for the teller; those who wish to work with traditional imagery may, as has been repeatedly shown in modern interpretations, find that it holds many keys to deeper consciousness.[1] This concept of keys to deeper or more potent levels of consciousness demands further consideration, as it is slightly different in the context of magical story-telling to that of direct meditation, prayer, or ritual magic.

We can approach the inherent power of magical tales from a historical or cultural viewpoint, but it must be emphasized that this is valuable only as a foundation, and not as a statistical or purely historical or academic thesis. In traditional story-telling, which is the basis for any modern redevelopment of magical tales, the teller frequently recounts material from ancient cultural levels or sources. These may have been preserved for many centuries through theme, motif, character, imagery, and through actual archaic language, poetry, and verbal units. A mixture of contemporary material with older strata in a story-teller's traditional repertoire does not in any way detract from the astonishing preservation of ancient lore and language . . . indeed, it emphasizes the inherent sacred quality of such lore that it remains honoured and enduring while contemporary matters come and go with each generation.

THE POWER OF LANGUAGE

In Ireland or the Western Isles of Scotland, we can find examples of twentieth-century story-tellers who recited long sagas from the heroic pagan Celtic era, handed down by word of mouth for many generations. Such story-cycles eventually vanish when an old native language, in this case Gaelic, is supplanted by that of a dominant culture. Indeed, there is an important connection between language and magical story-telling. The subtle implications and harmonic connections of traditional magical tales often do not survive translation, and certainly do not survive extensive changes of language within a community. The Creation of the World, which is the foundation of all magical tales, and the History of the Land and its Inhabitants, which is the development and poetic unification of such tales, may only be fully expressed in the original language of the people who generated and preserved their specific version of the tale.

We find this vital concept corrupted in the popular and wildly inaccurate use of Hebrew in occult literature, even though the great majority of occult writers were not Hebrew speakers or of Jewish origin. The key concept of a *sacred language*, known to all peoples in all places, had, from the late seventeenth century onwards, in literature dealing with magical techniques, become confused through religious orthodoxy and conditioning, a confusion which resulted in lamentable ignorance of organic or native esoteric, magical and spiritual traditions. This confusion is particularly apparent in the esoteric or magical texts of European writers in the nineteenth and early twentieth centuries, where misconceived and ill-understood Hebrew was freely mixed with Egyptian (then extremely fashionable) English, French, and occasionally other languages.

Even today in the late twentieth century, there is still a bizarre inaccurate tendency to assume that the West has no spiritual traditions other than orthodox Christianity, and that all deep insights must be imported from other cultures. This entire sorry situation lead us to the conclusion that if we are to use language and story-telling in an empowered manner today, we must be certain that we employ languages which are a true part of our innermost lives. Thus there is a strong spiritual, magical, and psychological case for the use of English for English speaking peoples, rather than a fantastical flight into superficially assimilated Hebrew, Sanskrit, Tibetan, or other languages, so often used as a type of trivially elitist technical vocabulary of symbolism, spiritual dialectic, or of mystique rather than mysticism.

In brief, our native tongue has the most potency and potential, whatever it may be. Material translated from different languages, however, may hold powerful images, concepts, and insights; such potencies are, of course, universal rather than linguistic, national, or racial. As has been touched upon above, subtle nuances from specific traditions can, unfortunately, be lost in translation; this is quite a different matter to loss of cultural cross-references or simple misunderstanding, and relates to the deep roots of language within consciousness.

THE DEEPER LEVELS OF MAGICAL STORY-TELLING

Oral traditions, reaching deep into the roots of a tribal or national past and the collective relationship with the land, are well attested by scholars world-wide, and are not in any sense rare or freakish cases. At one time, all people preserved such a pool of ancestral poetry, imagery, lore, history, and knowledge. Indeed, in non-literate cultures, living close to the environment, such tales were the sum of identity, wisdom, and insight for the collective national tribal or family group.[9] In certain individual cases — those of the dedicated magician, wise man or woman, or seer — such traditions were empowered to an even deeper level through special disciplines; but it is most significant that these initiatory arts employed the very same symbols as traditional tales and poems. In other words the keys to inner power were found to be the common property of all, and not by any means a reserved or exclusive secret.

We find this concept again in the Mystery religions of the ancient world, wherein well-known myths or tales were redefined and made the subjects of ritual drama and initiation. Despite the specialization and revelation, the foundational material was part of common consciousness . . . a legend, a hero, a group of gods and goddesses. Membership of a Mystery revealed esoteric or deeper levels of a myth or religion, and worked towards profound transformations using the symbols of such myths in an empowered manner.

It is important to realize that traditional tales arise simultaneously from both early levels of culture and deep levels of consciousness. In superficial terms, it appears that the further back we travel in time (in a story) the further we are delving into ancestral imagination and awareness. This is a very different picture to the factual viewpoint of history, yet ancient tales preserve in a dreamlike form, many matters that have been verified in terms of academic history or archaeology.

SACRED TALES AND TAROT

In Eastern cultures today, it is said that blessings are earned by reciting and listening to certain sacred epics. The same benedictive quality was consciously ascribed to certain early Irish tales, and is clearly described and asserted in monastic texts in which pagan tales were preserved, by orthodox Catholic monks and scribes, through their inherent traditional sanctity. Such long tales are always concerned with the creation of the world or worlds, and the adventures of the inhabitants, who range from gods and goddesses to heroes, humans, and animals.

A very similar pattern is found in the twelfth century *Vita Merlini*, which preserves a complex creation and adventure cycle woven around Merlin, drawn in part from Welsh or Breton bardic traditions by Geoffrey of Monmouth.[10] The Tarot, which seems to have first appeared in the form of illustrated cards in Italy during the Renaissance, is very likely to be drawn from such a story-telling or bardic cycle of images dealing with creation and transformative adventures.[3] Such blessed tales were originally found in all lands, but have now virtually died away in Western civilization. Thus if we are to reinstate magical tale-telling or tale-generation, it must fulfil certain basic requirements: a) to employ a living language and not be stuffed with false or exotic vocabulary, and b) to somehow fulfil the magical role of virtually lost oral traditions in a manner suitable for modern culture.

Interestingly, tarot fulfilled certain aspects of that role when it first appeared as formal picture cards, and they were used for story-telling in southern Europe for several centuries. Today there is a considerable revival of tarot, much of which is trivial, dull, or absurd. In this revival story-telling is once again being linked to tarot. If a traditional cycle of symbols, situations and characters from mythic tale-telling was the source of tarot, as seems very likely, then tarot provides one significant route back into that primal creative mode of consciousness.[11]

But we must be very wary indeed of using tarot for rule of thumb trivial exercises in assembling meaningless 'symbolic' narratives, just as we must take similar care not to prostitute the enormous potential of tarot into crude immature fortune-telling.

In this context of tarot and European story-telling traditions we might emphasize that the old tellers did not merely draw cards and talk through or improvize from the images that appeared. Each card or combination acted as a trigger, or sometimes as mnemonic, for portions of a vast oral repertoire already firmly established within the story-teller's memory and imagination. Perhaps the best known parallel might be the Ancient Greek epics of The *Iliad* and The *Odyssey* ascribed to Homer, in which many separate tales, motifs, and images were assembled together from traditional myth and legend by a master poet.

In the collection of original magical tales in this book, tarot images and structures are suggested in the introductions to a few of the stories, but they are not essential to reading, understanding, or enjoying the stories themselves.

MAGICAL TALES AND COLLECTIVE CONSCIOUSNESS

Although traditional tales were preserved by individual and highly respected tellers, they originated in what might be called a transpersonal realm or mode of awareness. This cannot be over-emphasized: there were no 'authors' of traditional magical tales; they were organic and anonymous. We might be strongly tempted to say that they were the products of the 'unconscious' as defined by Jungian psychology and other modern schools of the psyche, but although this definition is adequate and proper in its modern therapeutic context, it does not encompass, or even approach, the traditional magical tales and epic cycles of non-literate cultures. There is a profound distance and difference between the use of fictive improvization in therapy and the anonymous cosmological, magical, and initiatory tales preserved collectively world-wide.

The key to magical story-telling, with its undeniably therapeutic and transformative powers, is more likely to be found within esoteric psychology — those studies of human consciousness made and taught for millennia before our modernist revival and development of psychotherapy. Indeed, we can be more precise, and assert that one of the main keys to the power of magical tales lies in the *visualizing* of emblems or personae within them; other essential factors must also be present, but we can consider the importance of visual units briefly at this stage.

As mentioned briefly above, a major art in esoteric or inner development, regardless of school or religion, is *creative visualization*. It may be firmly limited and guided, as in Jesuit disciplines and certain Eastern religions, or it may employ a certain degree of free association set within a defined tradition. Such defined traditions are those of symbolic or imaginal 'alphabets', which are sets of gods and goddesses, other characters, attributes within a cosmology, and so forth. Esoteric arts and sciences use well-known sets, such as the Tree of Life, the Three Worlds, the Wheel of Life, or the Tarot, to great effect.

BARDS, POETS, AND THE POWER AND ART OF MEMORY

A process similar to the magical 'alphabets' but less defined and controlled was used by the old traditional story-tellers. This may be one of the reasons for their prodigious, almost unbelievable memories, for they often had enormous repertoires and could recite tales that lasted for hours or even days, and remember perfectly a story that had only been heard once, and retell it accurately many years later. Such feats of memory are well-attested by scholars, collectors, and researchers into tradition. But are they feats of memory in the modern sense, where one has to accumulate data in an order and then work to replicate that order in verbal and conscious patterns? Undoubtedly they are of a different order.

An example might help us to consider this link between visualization and memory, and how it applies to the transformative power inherent within magical story-telling. A tape recording made by the School of Scottish Studies, interviewing an old Gaelic story-teller, clearly defines his method of memory. He says (in Gaelic) that he remembers the tales because he sees them as pictures upon the wall — in other words as a projected and connected series of images. The images enabled him to regenerate the words associated with each image. Furthermore he had learned the tales by listening to a story-teller when he was young and attuning to the images, the pictures upon the wall. When he knew the pictures, the words came automatically, as if they could not be separated from one another.[12]

It is particularly interesting to note that the Gaelic story-teller projected the images 'upon the wall', as this is precisely one of the ancient techniques taught within magical and meditative schools, where the use of walls, mirrors, or the magical implements of the disc or shield, are all employed to give a field for the imaginative energies to become defined and active. We must remember that such examples from folk tradition are organic or innocent; there is no question of the tellers being part of a so-called 'occult' movement. In some localities, however, it would be reasonable to suggest they were the last remnants of an old bardic caste, particularly as tale-telling and ballad singing ran in specific families for many generations. The bards, in turn, were originally an order within the pagan Druid priesthood. In Ireland, Scotland, and some northern European countries, this definition of a special role for the poet and reciter of traditional lore was preserved well into the nineteenth and early twentieth centuries.

An organic unity was noted from traditional ballad singers in Britain and America by nineteenth and early twentieth century folklore and folk-song collectors; singers repeatedly asserted that the music and the long ballad stories were inseparable, and that to know one was to know the other.[13] The same is frequently found in the learning of traditional dances — to know the music is to know the dance steps. This is clearly 'remembering' of a very different type to that usually employed in education, and the unification or harmonic merging of images, music, dance steps and so forth is far too widespread and well-attested to be passed off as a mere matter of poor education or lack of explanatory ability on the part of ignorant participants.

The visual aspects of oral tradition, which link closely to magical imagery, with so many characters drawn from ancient religion and deep ancestral themes, have hardly been studied at all. There are many resonances of the classical art of memory formalized by the ancients, and preserved in a number of medieval scholastic texts. A detailed analysis of this art is found in Frances Yates's book *The Art of Memory*,[14] and there is certainly some connection between traditions of immense memory in story-telling, and a lost classical art which may have originally come out of the temples of the pagan world. The remnants of this system seem to have been directed towards oratory, but it has many implications of a more profound origin.

But we are not talking of a conscious orator's skill, we are dealing with an organic tradition rooted in primal magic; the images are not merely present as aids to memory, they are empowered magical images of gods, goddesses, heroes, adventures, other worlds and dimensions, and mysterious creatures. It is upon this level that magical story-telling may be reinstated for modern expansion of consciousness.

MODERN MAGICAL TALES

How, therefore, do we define or create and employ a magical tale for modern use? There is, of course, a considerable danger in attaching intellectual or systematic interpretations to stories, be they psychological, materialist, or esoteric. But despite this risk, there are certain specific functions or roles of the specifically magical tale which differ from those of stories in general fiction. As mentioned above, attuning to a tradition is perhaps the most important, and allowing that tradition to regenerate fruitfully and harmoniously within a modern style and literary or — far less common nowadays — spoken context. But there are other more specific requirements of a magical tale, which are often absent from modern fantasy, even when it claims an overtly 'magical' theme.

Perhaps the most curious and obscure example of these is that of attuning to other worlds and times. The hallmark is that we feel such worlds and times to be most real, not as a matter of suspension of disbelief, but in an intuitive and sometimes painful flow of recognition. In other words, certain magical tales are not symbolic, allegorical, poetic, or spiritually enlivened in the sense of wisdom tales or potent visualizations, they are instead windows into real places, real times, and real people. The magic is inherent not only in the connection between our imagination and those other worlds or times, but in the interplay between our consciousness and those places and people. This phenomenon is well-known in esoteric, spiritual or magical arts, though it is seldom discussed adequately, and may give rise to absurd claims and wild nonsense on the part of those who would like to be known for contacting other worlds, and therefore fantasize something exotic or grandiose to inflate their self-esteem.

IMAGES, VISUALIZATION, AND RITUAL

Magical tales were originally a collective route, a path towards inner transformation. They provided the reassurance, entertainment and education of well-established cultural traditions, but could, if required, be taken several steps further. Like the ancient Mysteries, they had an exoteric or outer meaning and function, and an esoteric or inner one. The paradox of true spiritual tradition, embodied in collective or oral traditions world-wide, is that the esoteric function is totally explicit in the outer form; there are no hidden schools of obscure interpretations or deep hidden secrets. Anyone making grandiose contact claims is unlikely to have attuned to a genuine tradition.

To create a magical tale for the modern reader or listener, the creator must tap into a genuine magical tradition, and not merely write about something quaint or 'magical'. To employ a modern magical tale, the reader or listener must build the images in his or her imagination; this is far more important than any intellectual assessment, though there is frequently and properly an intellectual level and substance to the symbolism and patterns in magical tales.

But esoteric literature abounds in recondite, obscure intellectual expositions, interpretations, methods, techniques, and theories. The magical tale, however, like the magical ballad or song, should act directly upon consciousness through its imagery, while the intellectual content operates not only through the logical processes, but transcends them by acting from a higher level of consciousness altogether. So it is possible to give keys to or interpretations of magical tales (as has been done briefly for each one in this collection), but the keys are not in any way essential to the magic or transformative force of the imagery, pattern, characters or events within the tale itself. Indeed, excessive interpretation can lessen the impact of magical tales; they are generated from and should speak directly to the deepest areas of the imagination regardless of interpretation.

There is a well-known and easily detected odour of falseness to things contrived by assembling 'symbolism'. Popular psychology has much to answer for in this respect, as is demonstrated extensively in many forms of commercial advertising, some 'psychologized' schools of novel writing or drama and screenplay, and in certain of the visual arts. Thus it is easy and eminently possible to assemble a good set of magical symbols into a plausible narrative, but this does not necessarily make a magical tale.

Like the creation of artificial life forms in popular fiction, the meaningful union of proper, even healthy parts does not make a living entity. The result is often a rotten corpse or a potentially dangerous monster. Once again, advertising or perhaps pop music videos give many examples of such potential pollution or enervation of the imagination.

One highly effective method of working with traditional magical tales and ballads, which may sometimes be applied to modern magical tales, is to take structural phases of the narrative and the visual images as sources for ritual pattern making. This is merely a more sophisticated version of the centuries old tradition of dancing or acting out narrative tales and ballads; it consists of applying the elements of the tale within the master glyphs of magic, such as the Fourfold Circle, or the Tree of Life, and generating a dramatic or ceremonial sequence from them.[8]

It should be emphasized most strongly that this technique is not the same as psychodrama or ritual enactment used in psychotherapy, and that it can lead to very powerful forces and deeply transformative experiences. Whereas role-play in psychotherapy or counselling may be beneficial in some cases, magical ritual taps into vast imaginative traditions enduring through many centuries, and has a number of very potent and well-established effects. Most important of all, magical ritual or ceremonial drama is not, and never has been, intended as 'therapy'; it forms one of the ancient techniques of willed inner transformation and redirection of vital energies, and usually demands that the operator or celebrant is as psychically mature and well-balanced as possible. Having said all of the foregoing, there are obviously many stages of development and levels of technique and ability between the two extremes of trivial therapeutic role-play and empowered ritual. Magical tales are one method of enlivening the psyche while avoiding some of the pitfalls inherent in either materialist psychology or esoteric arts.

After our brief discussion of the background to magical tales and the story-telling tradition, and our suggestions concerning a possible revival of this almost lost art in modern terms, let us move now to a selection of original magical tales. The stories which follow are not intended to cover the entire range of magical tale-telling; to do so would require a much larger volume. They are instead a selection of certain tales and themes which are intended to serve as an introduction to the art. Some are drawn from traditional themes, while others come from story-cycles and magical motifs which tap into a number of specific esoteric or innerworld contacts. But if all of the foregoing seems too portentous or demanding, then we need to remember only that they are first and foremost stories, entertainment, nourishment and stimulation for our imagination.

HOW A BOOK
WAS FOUND

In this tale we have two of the eternal characters; the wise old man and the foolish youth. They are found in folk-tales, oral tradition, and esoteric wisdom traditions world-wide. Unfortunately, the theme often becomes horribly stereotyped; the old man becomes a perfect elder master, while the youth becomes a potential hero, king, or saviour. Curiously the more idealized the characters are, the less effective the story. To balance this suggestion, which might well be disputed by many, we need only look at the older or primal strata of tales and myths, in which there are no 'perfect' beings; the gods, goddesses, heroes and heroines tend to show rough edges, failings, warts, and hangovers.

Some of these rough edges are, of course, the result of cultural changes as time passes; that which is acceptable to one age becomes unacceptable to another. The great Greek or Celtic gods and goddesses displayed immense sensuality, a force which was not at all acceptable to the Christian model of divinity. Yet today many people are seeking the deeper spiritual levels of paganism, which are often found through and beyond such sensuous images as the gods and goddesses of the ancient world. [15]

Reaching *beyond* the imagery is the key; but it must first be met head on and not side-stepped. Anyone who has examined oral traditions of entertainment, education, or wisdom tales will find them rough and ready, often harsh and violent. This harsh quality is also present in the deeper magical and spiritual traditions, but it is, regrettably, ironed out in commercialized or popularized presentations for the general student and reader. We might stand all of this argument on its head, and say more simply that anyone who claims to have met a shining angel, a perfected master, or to be instructed by a wise Merlin complete with pointed star-spangled hat and long white beard is either lying or deluding themselves. Those who have had deep experience of the magical transformative arts will affirm that the images and the personae met with in meditation, visions, and dreams have many peculiarities about them.

So while this tale might be about The Hermit and The Fool in tarot, or Merlin and the young Arthur in medieval legend, it has been set in the present day. The wise old man is a shell-shocked war veteran, while the boy is any callow young thing who runs away from home. The fact that neither of them manage to communicate with another in any way should not be too depressing; it was their meeting that was important, like the presence of two chemicals within a vessel, and not any intellectual content of their exchange of words.

It would be unfair to introduce this tale without referring briefly to some of the hidden traditions that it embodies. Only a generation or two ago, the subjects touched upon in this, and in several related tales in this book, might have been regarded as 'temple secrets', taught only to members of magical or esoteric groups when they were proven trustworthy. The late twentieth and early twenty-first centuries, however, demand a different approach, not least because many of the temple secrets have been so abused and prostituted by journalistic writers who have no true understanding of their meaning that they need to be set once again in simple form. That form is the *ludibrium* or totally ridiculous story which, despite its silliness, contains certain key images, sequences, or symbols that attune to magical or spiritual traditions.

The book, the tomb, the living illuminated letters, all described in this tale, are classic esoteric themes, found in folklore, religion, magical arts, and alchemy. More specifically, they crop up in the much-debated Rosicrucian traditions, which seem to have been derived in turn from a deliberate fusion of esoteric Christian sources with pagan Germanic, classical and Celtic tradition. The Gospel of Mary Magdalene, a central motif in the story, has occupied the minds of writers and thinkers for centuries, and has appeared in many tales, novels, and esoteric theses.

More specifically, it forms the foundation for a mystical tradition propounded by Robert de Boron in the Middle Ages, in which two children, a son and daughter born of Jesus and Mary Magdalene, were brought to Britain by Joseph of Arimathea, [16] possibly to Glastonbury, where a Druidic temple, probably to the goddess known to us as Brigit or Bride, preceded an early Celtic Christian monastery dedicated to the Virgin Mary. This is, remember, a mystical tradition, and there is no requirement that it be 'proven' in any way; indeed, obsessive pursuit of such proof is not only a waste of valuable energy and time, but clear evidence that the pursuer has not grasped the true value of the tradition itself. A certain amount of proof is helpful in the early stages of liberation from conditioning, especially that of religiously and politically tailored 'history', but it should not be an end in itself or it becomes a means of entrapment rather than a route to freedom.

Although much spurious fuss has been made about traditions of this sort in recent years by popular journalistic writers, they have been known and, I would stress, quite widely discussed and taught among esoteric religious and magical groups or movements for centuries. Indeed, they were current in the twelfth and thirteenth centuries, and stem back to pagan traditions of sacred bloodlines, so are hardly anything in the way of a shocking revelation. Intellectual assessment of these bloodline traditions is, however, fruitless; they must be encountered upon deeper and empowered levels of consciousness.

One last note; the tramp in this story was a real person; I met him and talked to him often before his unfortunate death at the hands of a driver while he was out upon his endless ramblings. Many of the words uttered by the character in this tale are exactly as I remember them; the discourse upon thunder and lightning, the time-jumping, the wandering around Britain from furthest north to south on foot, the sleeping in churches and graveyards, and, of course, the multiple watches. Back in the 1960s he was a last representative of a very specific type of itinerant; the shell-shocked veteran of the Great War of 1914-18. These men, some of them 'officers and gentlemen' were not able to live within society, or even indoors, after the horrors of trench warfare, and they took to the roads.

I doubt if any of them are left alive now. Yet they, in their terrible pain, suffered for their people and country in what was supposed to be the war to end all wars, so they are part of the deep mythology of the land. Did not Merlin run mad, unable to live with men, after a terrible battle in which his comrades were killed? Did he not go on to attune to the forces of the land, the animals, the stars in the heavens?[10] We might draw a comparison to the veterans of the Vietnam war, some of whom live in the wilds in America and Canada today. So real people, through their pain and suffering, take on mythic roles and potencies. That's why their story may be retold in many different forms, even as a ludibrium.

HOW A BOOK WAS FOUND

One day, a fairly long time ago, there was a young person, somewhere between boy and man. He foolishly set out to follow a road, not caring where it led him as long as it carried him away from his parental home, from his family no longer tolerable to him. Like many young men, he boldly wallowed in the assumption that he and he alone had the dynamic will to behave in such a dramatic and utterly original manner; he firmly believed that the road would lead him to a rich and rewarding new life. He took

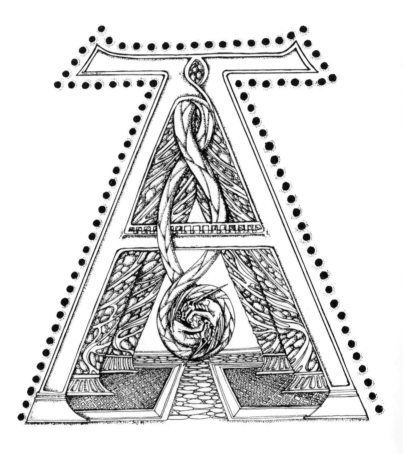

with him a pack containing a few clothes and books, a bedroll, and a mass-produced stringed instrument which he played badly.

If this youth had been able to rise vertically into the air, defying those natural laws which most successfully kept him in his proper place, he might have seen many curious things. The manner in which rivers and rain interact, for example, or the layers of filth buffeted about by the four winds which unsuccessfully scour the works of man. He might have seen the last remaining great beasts sporting in the oceans, or terrible wounds to the planet in hidden places, deserts, tiny islands. If he could have looked down upon the turning world, he might have particularly noticed a large number of other young men, setting out upon roads, clutching a variety of nasty noise-generating devices, and all with wild hopeful gleams in their eyes. But he was not able to rise in such a manner, and so saw very little to persuade himself that he was in no way unique or important.

Regrettably for our tale something quite unusual did, in fact, happen to this youth. We may assume that it happened by accident rather than design; furthermore the unusual quality of this event was greatly modified by the crude fact that he had no idea whatsoever that anything remarkable was taking place. He did nothing whatsoever to live up to or through the event, and soon forgot all about it. So in one sense our story confirms that he was merely a buffoon.

After several days of trudging stylishly through rain, stealing fruit from gardens, and occasionally pausing beneath trees to pluck at his instrument and emit nasal gargling sounds from his mouth, this youth came upon a large dilapidated barn. It seemed an ideal place to rest for the night, though the day was only halfway done, where he might work upon a song which he had been creating during his long walk over the hills towards the unseen coast.

Ducking in out of the wet, he failed to see that a curious emblem was carved over the stone lintel. The barn had once been a chapel or lesser house of a great abbey, but such things meant nothing to the youth, burning as he was with an inflated and spurious newness, brightness, revolution, and originality. The emblem which he did not see remained, nevertheless, true to its own existence. It would have been in that place if he had not passed that way, even if he had not been born; this fact makes his presence in the barn or chapel even more lamentable. The carving over the door was of two elegant tall vessels or pots, each with a serpent or dragon coiled around it, and the serpents' tails were interlinked.

Flinging himself ungracefully into a sprawling posture upon the rotten straw, this youth stared for a while at the roof, and at the holes in the roof, humming tunelessly to himself. Then, despite the obvious fact that there was no one present other than himself, he took his instrument out of its delightful plastic bag and set himself in a very creative and meaningful pose. In this considered stance, one leg raised with foot upon a stone, head flung back and shoulders hunched, he drew a shallow breath in through his mouth, and began to strum. As he plucked and thrashed the strings, his slightly bulging eyes urged open to their full width, and a wild stammering sound spurted from his loose lips. This was not, as you might think, his new song after all, but a natural response to something which he had suddenly seen in the distant corner of the barn.

Within the dusty shadows cast by late afternoon light seeping through the old tiles, a pile of straw and rags was moving, heaving up into a sinister shape, sprouting two arm-like extrusions, staggering and swaying towards him.

'I say, old boy' came a highly cultured voice 'Do stop that damned funny noise will you?' From out of the rags a dark brown shining bald head emerged, revealing the monster to be an elderly man wrapped in a greatcoat, with newspaper and straw stuffed in the arms and neck. He wore thick, faded green tweed trousers, heavy well-polished army boots. In short he was a tramp, or so it seemed at the time.

'Do you mind . . . I was trying to sleep.'

The youth put down his instrument muttering something concerning the relationship between creativity and oppression. He sat and looked for a moment at the tramp, who sat and looked at him. A strong ripe odour wafted gently but inexorably between them, as if the older man had rolled in dung, sweat, grass, cheese, earth, leather, stale bread, fried onions and beeswax.

'Well, no time left to sleep now I suppose, must be on my way before the thunder . . .' He paused and looked meaningfully at the youth, as if waiting for a question. 'What thunder, you may well ask? Well young man, I have been caught out in thunder before, and man must be outdoors, out from cover, rather than in a stone chapel with a timber roof'. The youth muttered something about no thunder, pouting and surly.

'Ah, well, not that you can see it yet, or hear it yet of course, but it *is* coming, believe you me . . . it is coming. Thunder.' The tramp sat and waited for a moment, watching his creative young guest drag stale bread and cheese from his damp pack.

'Would you be willing to spare a crumb of that food, perhaps?' The youth grudgingly passed some bread over, which was enfolded and squeezed in a large black grimy hand before being eaten. How could the voice of an army officer and gentleman issue from such a seedy wreck?

'Yes, thunder, on its way. Soon. Can't stay indoors y'know, thunder, rather like gunfire . . . what?' At the word gunfire his grimy hands shook, and the faded bright blue eyes closed for a few seconds. 'But you look like a clever young man, probably had some education . . . now what would you say to the fact that, not a mile from here, I found something of immense, no not immense, inestimable value? And what would you say if I told you that something was still buried beneath a slab of stone in a graveyard? What would you say to that eh?'

The youth chewed his bread and mumbled something original, witty and caustic to the effect that there were more valuable things in life than buried treasure. The tramp smiled gently at this, and looking through and beyond his guest continued to talk as if to no one in particular . . . or perhaps to the person who the youth might one day become.

'Yes, on my travels I find many strange and interesting things . . . people do throw out the most useful items, perfectly adequate watches, the water that eggs have been boiled in, the best parts of bread. But this was not thrown out, definitely not, for it was *hidden*.' He paused and his eyes suddenly snapped back into focus, demanding a reply. But just as the youth was about to ask a question, the tramp interrupted: 'Do you happen to have the right time, old boy?' Confused at this deliberate disruption of what was already an abnormal conversation, the youth took his plastic watch from his pocket. He muttered that it might be around four thirty, but he did not believe in keeping track of time, so the watch could be wrong.

'Ah, well I *do* believe in keeping track of time, yes indeed. Good time keeping is the key to a productive and meaningful life; as you get older you'll realize the truth of what I say.'

As he spoke the tramp struggled to push up the left sleeve of his greatcoat, shedding straw, strips of newspaper, and what seemed to be faded photographs. He finally uncovered a shirtless brown arm, and an elegant gold wrist-watch, above which was another watch of a different design. Neither watch showed the time to be four thirty. Then, to the youth's callow amazement, the tramp pushed up his right coat sleeve, revealing three more watches: a schoolboy's plain old-fashioned one with a thin leather strap, a diver's with a thick steel rim and many buttons and numbers, and an immensely valuable Rolex. Upon each watch he conducted a slow ritual of correction, affirming the necessity for good time-keeping. When he had finished, none of the watches showed four thirty . . . indeed, the youth was almost sure that they did not work at all.

'Good. Now where was I? Oh yes, in the chapel talking to a boy about thunder. Well, I stay outside when it thunders. Much the safest place to be y'know. Sometimes I sleep in the churches, but nowadays most of them are locked, which is damn strange if you ask me. It's those radical new Bolshevik clergymen getting up to monkey tricks . . . the house of God should be open to all comers, not padlocked like some bloody counting house. Do you know young fellow, that in Salisbury they have a turnstile at the door of the Cathedral? What would the founder of their religion make of that little device, I ask you?

'So when it thunders I stay outside because the force of the storm is dissipated, spread, you see, and not contained or amplified by the vessel of the building. Particularly if it is a church. You probably know that those old churches were built to collect, as it were, the energies of nature. Well for centuries they were blasted and knocked about by lightning until some clever chap invented the lightning conductor. But those lightning conductors only reroute electricity, which is the power that you can see . . . they do nothing whatsoever for the power that you can't see, if you see what I mean.' At last he paused, waiting for a reply, and when the youth remained sitting in stunned silence, the tramp's eyes clouded over and he seemed to lose interest.

Thinking that the lecture was over at last, the youth began to pluck artistically at his instrument, producing a confused thrashing sound similar to that of an egg-whisk rapidly beaten up and down across a set of bedsprings. The tramp reached out a long arm and wrapped a very large hand around the strings, muffling them utterly. The stink was overpowering; the youth leant back, reluctant to breathe, but even more reluctant to relinquish his source of creative fulfilment, wealth and fame.

'So there I was safe in the graveyard where the thunder and

lightning could do me no harm. I sat there and watched the storm, wondering what the right time might be. You can set your watches by those storms, y'know, if you happen to know what the right time is to start with. As I sat there, a large bolt of visible lightning struck a nearby sepulchre, dating I would hazard from the twelfth century or thereabouts . . . the sepulchre that is and not the lightning. This is why time-keeping is so important, but my watch seemed to have stopped that day.

'It was a particularly fine piece of work, that tomb. It had a bold carving of a knight, his hound, a hawk, a weeping woman who was probably the knight's sister, as they were all vowed to chastity in those days . . .' The tramp paused and waited for the youth to challenge him upon the subject of chastity, as if he knew that his suggestion was nonsense and had thrown it in merely to test his listener's lack of concentration.

'Hmmm . . . well, the slab collapsed, as it happened, leaving a hole rather similar to one in which I spent some time. That was back before you were born, that hole . . . quite a few years ago, actually . . .' The youth tried a tentative tug at his instrument, but the hand that held it was inflexible. The tramp did not seem to notice the attempt, his eyes were set upon some distant horror that left him silent for several minutes.

'What? You want to know what was in that hole in the grave-yard?' The youth had said nothing. 'Well, I'll tell you, but all in good time, all in good time and right order. First of all there was a flight of steps . . . steps! Someone, I said to myself as the rain poured down, has built a chamber under there, and down those steps I went. They led to a little wooden door with a bear carved upon it; damned old door, grey like stone, of English oak centuries old. They used to smoke it or pickle it, y'know, tough as steel, outlive any foreign wood you might care to name.

'Now I never go indoors during a storm, far too dangerous with all the thunder and the energy and all that. But the rain stopped, and the storm had passed, and as the next storm was several days away according to my watch, I felt reasonably safe and pushed the door in. It was rusted off its hinges of course, the wood outlasted the metal as it always does. In it fell and in I went.' The monologue ceased suddenly, the hand locked around the neck of the instrument slid away. To the youth's surprise a loud rasping snore uttered forth, and the tramp rolled over slowly into the dirty straw, asleep.

During that period of snoring, the youth packed his bag,

stuffed the instrument into its case, and rolled up his sleeping kit. He was about to creep out when he realized that it was dark, for night had arrived. He heard the bedtime bellowing of cattle singing one another to sleep, the distant purring of a tractor going home. For a moment he almost felt that he too would like to go home. In the barn, snoring was punctuated by muttered words, commands, tiny shouts that seemed to come from a vast distance away through the sleeper's open mouth.

Resting his head upon the instrument, the youth tried to sleep also. The old man's ridiculous tale drifted through his head, and he wondered what all the watches were for. Just as he slipped into a dream in which pale-faced meaningful young ladies complimented him upon his metaphors and his nimble fingering, he was rudely awakened by the loud voice of the tramp, suddenly speaking up as if no break had occurred in his conversation.

'So there I was in that chamber. It was pretty dark, about as dark as it is in here in fact, but there was just enough light to set your watch by, though not much more. If I'd had a luminous watch, for example, there would have been too much light for it to shine, but just enough to see the hands without them shining in the dark. Do you follow my line of thought? Good, I knew you would.

'Now I've been in Africa, France, parts of Asia, I've spent a lot of time walking around Britain from the far north of Scotland down to Cornwall. I know quite a few unusual things, most of which I hardly ever think about. I happen to know that it is more dangerous to be inside a church during a storm than it is to be outside. Very few people know that, believe you me. So I searched around and laid my hand upon a chest . . . a wooden chest. Damn thing fell apart, probably some exotic wood chosen for the colour or the scent or the rarity or something similar. Seven hundred years or so can do a lot of damage to some feeble foreign wood imported to please a greedy abbot or an effeminate prince!'

Again the voice stopped. The youth waited, knowing that the story would never end, fearing that he would be trapped in a barn forever listening to monologues about thunder or the relative qualities of British against foreign woods.

'Anyway I laid my hands upon an object, wrapped in rags of old leather, old and tough. Underneath there was good oiled leather, again and again in layers, and each layer was more whole than the one before it. Finally there was a wrapping of silk, real

old spider's silk such as was made before Chinese cloth was
carried over the long trade route from the East.

'I pulled that package out of the chamber and climbed back
up to the graveyard. What happened then? I hear you ask. Well,
I'm an old man, so I fell asleep.'

The barn was dark now, and in the sudden respite of silence,
the tramp produced a stump of candle from his deep pockets,
and setting it upon a block of stone between himself and the
youth, struck a match. The yellowish light flickered back and
forth, casting distorted shadows as the night wind breathed
through many holes in the roof. Then the candle was lit, and
over it the tramp placed a broken glass jar, to form a little lamp.

By this lamplight the youth saw for the first time fine arched
windows, long infilled with rubble stone. He saw remains of
carven faces high up towards the crude timber roof frame, and
mouldings and chequered patterns running high around the
walls. It was as if daylight, ample enough for seeing all things,
had not been as penetrating as this limited central light around
which stories were told. With this half-formed realization, the
youth waited patiently for the first time in his short life.

'Next morning, about 5 a.m., 7.33 a.m., or 10.19 a.m., I awoke
to find myself still clutching the package. In the sunlight I
unwrapped the plain grey silk covers to find a large hand-written
book, bound in a faded cover of tooled hide. Now if you had
found it, lad, could you have read it? What I'm saying is this; it
was in medieval Latin script . . . that horrid church Latin. Some
beautiful illuminations or illustrations, showing the strangest
scenes, but all written in that horrid crabbed script with the 'n's
and 'u's left open-ended so you could not tell the difference
between them.

'Well, I was never much of a scholar, but I had Latin beaten into
me at school like everyone else, and I did spend some time
studying between balls and parties and social events at Oxford.
So I could see straight away that this was some old monkish
gospel, probably a late copy, but perhaps even older than it
looked. Might have been hidden at the time of destruction and
dissolution of the great monasteries. The tomb seemed even
older than the book, but then I'm no expert or archaeologist, so
I just opened the covers to find out what it was all about. There
was the title, as bold and vivid as the nose on your face: The
Gospel of Mary Magdalene.'

At this, the youth stretched up from his customary slumped

position, for even he knew that there was no such gospel named after Mary Magdalene. He realized at last that this was a crazy old man's fantasy. But the tramp, not waiting for an incredulous response, began speaking again.

'Now I know that you're thinking that I'm a silly old chap who makes things up, just because in your King James Bible at school there never was any such gospel. Have you never heard of the Apocryphal Books? Do you know that there were many gospels suppressed or destroyed during the political growth of the Church? Ha! You know so little . . . you don't even know about thunder and lightning . . . outside, outside is safest when the power strikes down to earth. Outside.

'So, this Gospel of Mary Magdalene. A marginal note told me that it had been copied from an ancient scroll once in the possession of Saint Blaidydd, who in case you don't know, was the original Celtic saint who founded the local abbey. As the sun rose, by about midday, I had examined many of the pages, and read a few parts of the text. There were lots of references to a boy and a girl who owned two vessels or pots, though sometimes it seemed as if the children *were* the pots. Little wonder it died out as a serious religious book . . . Mary Magdalene was a loose woman you know, a harlot. Take my advice lad and steer clear of such women . . . for they will break you down.' With this curious statement, the tramp paused and stared off into the deep shadows. For a moment he seemed about to laugh at what he saw, but instead he immediately began to speak again.

'As I was saying, there were text and illustrations together. Those pictures were very elaborate, with letters, animals, fantastic beasts and birds that seemed to leap right off the pages at you, coloured red with powdered stone, and blue with lapis, and gold with fine bright golden leaf. I spent more time looking at the pictures than I did with the Latin script, I can tell you.

'There was one full page of a tree, growing upside down, with many strange creatures living in its branches. First of all I thought that the vellum had been bound wrongly into the book, but when I turned it around, the animals were upside down and so were the letters dotted around the branches like fruit. An upside down tree, with its ochre roots in a blue and silver shining sky, and its green leaves touching the rich red earth, balancing at last upon one slender central shoot.

'Another page showed what seemed to be a woman crucified, or perhaps it was a beautiful youth with long fair hair. But he or she was somehow free of the cross, no nails or ropes, and seemed to come forward towards me out of the picture with a smile such as I had not seen since . . . since a long time past.' For a moment he paused as if in memory, and then continued.

'Everything in that book reminded me of something else, and had more than one meaning. There were the capital letters that opened each page . . . the letter O became a cave seen from the inside looking outwards, out into the light. On this page I could make out some of the script, which seemed to say *"Seek out the resurrected body reborn forever."* Then there was the letter A which the scribe had shaped into the vault of a great cathedral. You looked down the long aisle, and it was all coloured with gold and green leaves, just as the churches were in the old days, gilded and painted to look like a spring or summer forest, with faces and beasts peeping out of the foliage painted and carved about the pillar and on the walls. But in the centre, where the crossing would be, where they would have had a central altar, was something quite different. In the heart of that tiny letter and picture was a great double dragon, coiled around a jewel, filling the centre of the cathedral and reaching up into the unseen tower above. On this page I read *"The Anointed One passes to and fro between the Throne and the Void. Rejoice ye all that he is at the centre of all things."*

Then there was the capital I like a great carven pillar with a fruitful vine curling up it, and the words *"He smote upon the Pillar of the Temple crying Cursed be they who seed the Mother Earth with burning stars to make her weep. Her pain shall return to them a thousandfold through many generations in the times and worlds to come."*

'Each vowel had its own tiny detailed picture as a capital letter. U was a cup or chalice, perhaps the Holy Grail . . . E had angels climbing up and down its branches, as if it was a ladder. I turned to the very end of the book, to read the final words. There was something about a band of travellers setting off westwards, then a different clear hand had added a marginal note: *"And some say that the two vessels dispersed their bounty throughout these blessed islands, so to this day do we bear their symbols as our arms, knowing likewise that two vessels and two dragons live within each man and woman."*

'Then another scribe had added the last words, squeezed into the bottom right-hand corner of the page: *"Guard you the innocents from all who shun charity, from all who close doors, from all who live without joy or grace. Such are the words of Mary of Magdala who speaks of her great love to those living at the closing of the Second Age. Such is also our word for the protection of this her Gospel, even unto the Fifth Age after which a new revelation shall arise in the hearts of men and women.''*

'Well, it was all beyond me, being a simple straightforward, no nonsense sort of chap much like yourself . . .' The tramp paused to observe the youth's response to this bizarre comparison, but as his listener was about to speak, he continued.

'So I thought I'd better take the book to the local vicar. After all it was in his grave, if you see what I mean, and those old abbey ruins were his patch, on his patrol. I wrapped it all back up in the old silk and leather, and walked over to the vicarage, which is about three miles from where we sit now, providing you are not distracted or side-tracked in any way. Yes, I've travelled widely in my time, and good manners mean a lot to me. I would say that next to accurate time-keeping, it is good manners that make the British people civilized. I cannot stand an ill-mannered person . . . least of all an ill-mannered woman.'

The tramp fell silent, and after some minutes had passed, the youth assumed that the old man slept again. His bulky square shoulders and round shining head seemed immobile in the faint lamplight. A rat squealed and scurried in the straw, there were night noises as the roof beams settled and moved to their own secret pattern. But the youth was now fascinated by the story, and opened his mouth to speak, hoping to awaken the teller. He had hardly drawn breath when the tramp spoke up briskly, as if he had never paused.

'So what about good manners I hear you ask? And you are right my boy, to ask such a question . . . I admire your perception. Well in my younger days, and if it had been a man, I might have thrashed him. But this was a woman, and bad manners in women have always puzzled me. So I knocked upon the vicarage door, and out came the vicar's wife. "Good day ma'am", I said, and she gave me that suspicious look that means No Cup of Tea Here. "Good day ma'am, and might the vicar be at home?" "No, yes," she says . . . damned if I see how he can be out and in at the same time. So I hold up the book and she sort of flinches back . . . "I have found this book ma'am, in the nearby parish graves. I wish to place it in your husband's safe keeping." I take a step forward, and she slams the door in my face! Slam! In my face!

'I look at the time, and it is 3.33 p.m., or 5.42 p.m., or 7.29 p.m.

and I think that the vicar was a tomfool to marry such an ill-mannered hussy. Right, says I to the book, back you go. So I walked back to the graveyard, but by a different road. Took three or four days I think, and there was some thunder about. When I got back there, I stuffed the Gospel of Mary Magdalene into that little chamber where it had hidden for all those centuries, and pushed the door shut hard. Lasts forever that pickled English oak, nothing like it in the world. Then, just to spite her, the vicar's wife that is, I spent a day or so pushing earth back into the hole with my bare hands.

'No one uses that graveyard now, they have a new place over by the housing estate, and no one saw me at work. No one ever sees me at work. Not long after that it was time to head North, about 8.24 a.m. on a Monday with the weather dry and no sign of thunder. Never saw that book again. Might still be there for all I know. The Gospel of Mary Magdalene.'

And with these words the old tramp rolled over and slept. This time he did not snore, but twitched and muttered his way through bad dreams. The youth extinguished the lamp, and crept away into the early dawn. A few stars were shining and the road glowed with that pearl light that comes before the rising sun. He walked away, glad now to have made his escape. By sunrise he had caught a lift right through to the city, forgetting all about the sea that he had originally aimed for. He never thought about the chapel, the old man, or the hidden book, again.

THE GIFT THAT CANNOT BE REFUSED

This tale contains some of the traditions found through visualization or meditation upon a magical or metaphysical location known as The Mysterious Abbey.[2] In essence, there is a mysterious building or foundation, which is said to exist in another dimension. It takes the form of a curious abbey, often with doorways within it that lead to other types of temple. It is not orthodox Christian, neither is it entirely pagan. One branch of the Order which serves in this abbey is involved with a perpetual cycle of tale-telling: these are the people upon whom this story focuses.

Readers familiar with English history will find a vague parallel to the suppression of the monasteries ordered by King Henry VIII. The last Abbot of Glastonbury, reputedly the most ancient Christian settlement in Britain, was ignomiously hung from a tree; the great library of Malmesbury Abbey, holding a huge collection of irreplaceable texts, was destroyed or dispersed; and for many years the townsfolk used the vellums for domestic purposes such as rolling into barrel bungs. I would stress that these interesting correlations are not the main purpose of the tale, but are merely asides.

Visualizations within the story

As one of the sub-themes of 'The Gift that Cannot be Refused' is tale-telling, it opens many doors or reveals many mirrors leading to other stories or cycles of stories. For the reader who wishes to pursue such themes in visualization, I would recommend some imaginative work with the abbey, the carvings over the fireplace, and the deep crypt in which the tales are endlessly retold.

The variant of a familiar riddle that appears towards the close of the tale, that of the Song that Cannot be Sung, the Bell that Cannot be Rung, the Book that Cannot be Written, or similar, is also found in many folk-tales. I must however, acknowledge Heather Brown, a visionary artist of considerable skill, who outlined to me a dream which forms the basis of that part of the story.

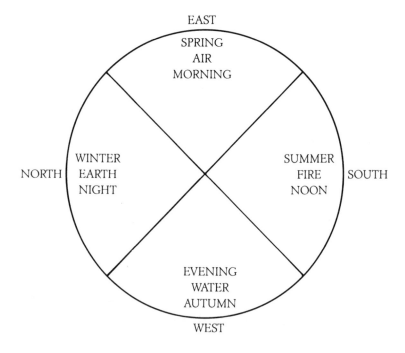

Figure One: The Fourfold Circle of Elements, Seasons, and Directions

Tarot images and patterns

In tarot images, the story attunes to a fourfold circular layout similar to Figure One using the Knight of Swords (East), the Hermit (West), Justice (South), and the Blasted Tower (North). The cards relate to one another across the circle, East-West, North-South, and sunwise around the circle, commencing with the East and travelling E–S–W–N. Patterns of this sort play on important and frequently misunderstood role in magical and meditational arts; in the present context they may be seen as the key patterns for the narrative and interaction of characters, but upon a deeper level they represent a cycle of transpersonal energies within any individual, leading to inner transformation.

In the *Merlin Tarot*[3] the Knight is known as the Warrior of Birds, and may be male or female, being disguised by a mask. In most tarot decks Knights are typified as male, but may also represent certain male qualities within a female. Like all tarot people or Court cards, this image is not rigidly fixed, but represents an archetype empowered by Elemental energies (Air, Fire, Water, or Earth); such archetypes and energies act as foundations for the personality. Thus the warrior in this tale has corrupted his energies towards negative ends, but another such person might employ them in a manner beneficial for humanity. In both cases the energies are those of Air manifesting through an active restless individual, Air of Air, Sword and Warrior.

The three Trumps of Hermit, Justice, and Blasted Tower stand respectively, in this tale, for the abbot, the challenge to the abbey and its response, and to the conclusion of the tale, in which 'The Gift that Cannot be Refused' is finally proffered.

THE GIFT THAT CANNOT BE REFUSED

In the library writing-room, the scribe paused and rubbed his eyes. Rain beat against the tiny glass panes of the window, candles smoked, and the letters seemed to suddenly crawl across the page. Putting down his pen he looked again at the wide vellum upon which he worked. It contained the story of the Blessed Youth, telling of his long time imprisoned in a hostile place. Each metrical paragraph opened with a decorated letter, while the page itself was graced with a large capital soon to be gilded and brightly coloured.

Wind rattled the edge of the window frame, suddenly diverting the scribe's attention; in that curious moment of distraction it

seemed as if the larger letter swirled into a shape, a pattern just beyond perception. It was suggestive of a road, of a thread travelling at speed along that road.

The scribe blinked, the page came into focus on the lines *'The right gift alone will defend against the powers that rage to destroy. No strength of arms or force of will shall defend you, only the gift that cannot be refused.'* He meditated for a moment upon the sacred tale, which related how a band of men and women had sought for that mysterious gift which might appease the captors of the Blessed One; how the youth himself had been upon a quest to steal a certain tree from an interior place within the Earth . . . until he was imprisoned wrapped in heavy blue chains.

To rest his eyes the scribe now looked about the long high room, as he had been taught. Panelled wood rubbed to a dark rich sheen spoke of peace, of discipline in art; but beneath these first words was found another tongue, which spoke of wisdom. Here in this room were written and preserved great books, intended to communicate the incommunicable . . . to percolate wisdom through and beyond the short lifetimes of mere men and women. With every retelling of the great story-cycle, a tiny fragment might change, and it was the dedicated work of scribes to note such changes and add them to the great volumes in the library. This library grew slowly and inevitably as a great tree through the centuries.

In a chamber far below the abbey, a group of brethren sat telling tales from memory, an endless recital punctuated by surges of song and chant. When one brother came to the end of his period of telling, another took his place. The chamber was circular; around the outside of the circle four listeners were appointed, no less important than the tellers themselves. The task of the listeners was to note down tiny changes as they arose within the story-cycle.

No one could say how such changes occurred, for each brother spent many years learning each tale to perfection, through rigorous discipline in mnemonic techniques and visualization. Yet, in the telling, changes arose spontaneously, without the conscious awareness of the tellers. They chanted on, lost in endless rhythm of the great tale that enfolded all lesser stories. When changes occurred, the listeners noted them and passed their notes onto the scribes for correlation, for entry into a relevant book or books. From this stage the material went to library masters for commentary, cross-reference, notes and learned disquisition.

Only three moons past a major sequence had suddenly been uttered, a whole new tale in which an innocent child was protected by the shielding magic of a spider's web. No one had heard this motif before, and it was immediately designated for transfer into the great books. Only a very few of the oldest brethren, frail and resting, muttered about the delicate tracery of webs carved high in the abbey roof . . . but in the joy of recording a new tale, no one heeded them. Their time was over. Soon the senior brothers would begin to comment upon this new tale during meal times, and everyone would then meditate upon it for the rest of the long winter. Curiously the child saved by the spider was not a boy, but a girl.

Soldiers cursed and muttered in the wet; forty men on foot and eight on horses. Cold seeping rain blew into their faces, driven by wind urging down the road towards them, funnelling out of the trees. Dark, steep and slippery, the way led upwards through the forest to their unseen destination. Water ran down hard iron helmets, chain shirts, thick leather trousers, into heavy nailed boots.

The forty foot-soldiers carried long pikes, finding it impossible to keep any measure of step on the irregular, shadowy road surface. In the chill they fell, stumbled and butted one another, prodding and bruising with the sheathed pike heads. Forced to keep up with the riders they plunged into a sullen murderous rage, burning for violence.

The focus and origin of their rage lashed his horse, spurring, forcing it over the rocks and rubble until it seemed that its hooves might bleed. Wrapped in a oiled leather cloak lashed tight around his waist, and wearing a crested padded helmet, he leaned forward into the road, desperate to reach his goal. As he rode his hands clenched and twitched upon the reins, opening and closing in spasms. His long nose and staring eyes jutted out into the wet night, his will leaping ahead of his straining body. And if the body kicked and spurred the horse, another less visible rider kicked and spurred the man, feeding his obsession to destroy.

Officers and men hated him; he drank up their hate, funnelling it through his own, using it to drive the troop through rising forestland into unknown shadows deep with winter. In his inner vision his loathing and rage poured ahead along the forest track . . . a message, a force, a forerunner of the physical threat that clattered, slithered and cursed along behind him in the troop of men.

If he was hated, he was also feared; men had been lashed with barbed whips as punishment; others had been drilled mercilessly by sergeants in bizarre methods devised by their commander, unheard of in regular training. If a man longed to skewer that distant mounted figure leading the troop, he also feared to come within spear's length of him.

Just as the troopers' rage was founded upon discomfort and fear, so was the darker hatred of their commander founded upon terror . . . so deeply buried that it seldom leaked through into his firmly marshalled outer thoughts. He had built a long career upon convoluted self-perpetuating anger, reinforced with callous self-interest, loathing any compassion. Yet this rigid, tense display hung above a void of terror. To appease that which whispered within he passed the terror onwards, feeding and instilling it into others. He regarded these victims as inferior, lower, weaker breeds; fear flowed through him into others and hardly seemed to touch him as it flowed. As the terror fed upon him, so did he feed upon all men and women he encountered — insatiable, unending, starving.

In his own chamber the abbot sat beside a warm fire. The season was remarkably cold and wet, and his advanced age had left him susceptible to damp. Resting after the evening ritual, resonances of chant still swirling through mind and body, he sat with eyes half-closed. An unseen watcher might have thought that he slept, but of the many unseen watchers that congregated within and around the abbey, no presence arose within the abbot's chamber. All such eyes were attentive elsewhere.

The fireplace was of stone, carved with a most elaborate sequence of images, made fluid and alive by a master mason long ago. Here could be seen a man falling out of a tree, head downwards into a swirling river; another apparently wrenching antlers from the head of a stag upon which he rode; a woman smiled secretively as she brushed leaves from her hair. These strange figures and scenes led into one another, surrounding the fire itself, some carved into the fireback where they might never be seen. The abbot remembered too clearly a small boy who had scrambled up the great chimney following the carvings into the sooty dark . . . himself almost ninety years ago. Through his eye-lashes as he rested now, he could just see a figure sitting cross-legged, begging perhaps. Beneath this figure was carved a hoard of coins and cups.

This central image of the beggar, dominating the keystone of the fire-arch, had been the subject of endless debate and re-search. But not one of the carvings appeared in any great tale; no researcher had found reference to them within the volumes of the library, not even in those oldest texts written in a language clouded with multiple levels of meaning. It was generally as-sumed that the fireplace was the work of a madman, perhaps set as a labouring penance for some unspeakable offence against rightness. A few elder brethren, more aged than the abbot him-self, muttered that in their childhood there was a teaching concerning the sequence of carvings; it was a prophecy, they said. It showed parts of the Great Story that would appear in the future. This doddering absurdity was ridiculed by the scribes, who held that such images were far divorced from the major symbols of the known tales. How could they, therefore, relate to any aspect of the Great Story that included all others . . . for the cycle evolved slowly out of itself, and even the unknown future must relate to the known past.

One thing was known; the fireplace had been a subject for dissension over a long period of time. During some distant past century a whole panel had been chipped away; it bore the marks of fervent styli where a group of scribes had presumably as-saulted an image in a fit of sacred devotion to truth. The mauled carving had not been restored or replaced, but left in its damaged state as a message . . . though no one could tell now what it was supposed to convey. All that remained of this lost image was what seemed to be the left foot of a bear.

After his long customary perusal of the fireplace, the abbot did indeed begin to drift into gentle sleep induced by firelight and age. As he drifted, he heard a curious gentle scratching at his door, and instantly sat up, awake. Seldom did the watchers come to him direct . . . he could hardly remember the last time that he had heard that sound, so small yet undeniable. This, he knew, was an important visitation. The abbot stood in acknow-ledgement, and a shadow moved across the wall as the door opened . . .

Breaking out of the trees at last the soldiers slid and cursed to a stop. Horses steamed, men groaned, sergeants looked about and fingered their weapons. Just ahead of the troop, their commander stared uphill, rigid upright in the stirrups.

Near now, partly hidden by a fold of land, stood the abbey church. Wind blew straight from it, driving rain into the faces of the waiting soldiers. The abbey was dark, almost purple-black, tinted by hints of pale moonlight scattered through flying clouds. From a massive central circular building, high spires and buttresses leaped to a square tower, surmounted by a tall sharp spire that pierced the clouds streaming over the hills beyond. Within the arched windows tiny lights could be seen, flashes of bright colour reflecting from glass, sparking and immediately dying away. This kaleidoscope fascinated the watching man for a moment . . . then he spat into the mud.

Now was his potent moment; he and he alone carried the commission to destroy this nest of fantasy. He visualized the weak shufflers within, pasty white faces mumbling incoherent drivel. He saw wealth piled in every corner, gathered from mock charity and spurious claims of teaching, healing. What the people needed was a firm head, authority to look up to, to fear . . . not this lying insipid weakness. In a little while he would ride up to the gate set within that high boundary wall, and make his demand, backed by the strength of forty-eight trained thugs, weapons, hatred, and the inestimable power of a long grudging march through winter night rain.

This was the time of reckoning, his personal reward for services in pursuit of power; the most effective commission had been granted correctly to the most effective man. The abbey held its lands upon an ancient condition, little understood, fallen into abeyance. Indeed, it had been virtually forgotten until one of the commander's spies had ferreted it out of an apparently insignificant legal document. This contained a charter setting out certain conditions, originally preserved by word of mouth, carrying a weight of royal authority unchanged through the centuries.

Lengthy debates had followed the unearthing of this charter, spurred and envenomed by one man's loathing of an ancient abbey and all that it represented. The basic terms of the deed were simple and incomprehensible; the crown or its representative could demand immediate bestowal of 'the gift that cannot be refused'. If such a gift was not forthcoming, all abbey lands and benefits were forfeit without appeal. The Order would be disbanded on pain of death. The material benefits of this forgotten old charter did not escape the crown and court; it had been reasoned shrewdly that the one man capable of refusing any gift whatsoever was he who now approached the abbey. Had he not brought the charter to the royal attention in the first place?

The abbey gate and gatehouse were set into a high deep wall. Within great double doors a lesser single door was set. The double doors had not been opened within living memory, nor did any record exist of their opening; they were sealed tight with age, rust, and a profusion of tiny plants that blossomed for the bees in summer. The single door was tightly bolted against the winter night, and no light shone in the gatehouse window.

Upon arrival, it took beating, cursing and pounding with pike-staves before a tiny grill opened high above the gate. A quavering voice asked what business transpired on such a gloomy night and in whose name. Enraged that he could detect no monkish face to accuse, the commander declared his royal warrant and demanded to meet with the abbot instantly. At this remarkable request a slightly larger grill in the single door, below that first tiny hatch, ground open slowly. Out of a mere slit of an opening, another voice declared itself to be the senior gatekeeper, asking what the renowned soldiery required.

The demand for the abbot himself was repeated, accompanied by a chorus of jeers and curses from the troops. After some time, much pounding, denting, swearing and shouting, the upper part of the single door (that part which contained the second hatch) was swung open the width of a mere crack. A third unseen person declared himself to be the steward of the abbey; he would be pleased to convey the request concerned to the abbot.

Seething with rage, forcing his voice into a measured tone calculated to inspire fear, the commander finally declared the purpose of his mission.

'As appointed representative of crown and state, rightful owners of the land on which you rest, I have come this night to claim the rightful due in payment of your rental, long neglected. I demand of you upon pain of total forfeiture, the agreed price, which is, in short, The Gift that Cannot be Refused.'

The half-door closed, and a scurrying of feet was heard. Soon a horn blew in the distance over the high abbey walls, and one by one the great arched windows of the church came alight. As he waited, the commander reflected upon humiliations that he might inflict upon this tardy arrogant abbot. Perhaps he could simply hang the charlatan from a nearby tree while the abbey burned . . .

The soldiery meanwhile had slumped down, allowed a brief rest by their sergeants. In time-hallowed manner they began to pick their noses, rub their crotches, and to inscribe graffiti with their knives into the wood and stone around them. There would be rations aplenty, they were told, when the abbey was taken.

Amid the consternation, rushing to light lamps kept in readiness but unused for centuries, whispered conversations and rapid consultations of rare texts, the tale-telling proceeded. Deep in the circular chamber below the abbey the story unfolded, unbroken, undiminished, unconcerned. The four appointed listeners took occasional notes, hardly realizing that they were not relieved at the usual hour. Such an interesting variant was growing out of the last chant . . .

Finally the entire single door opened, revealing the abbot robed in white and gold, with a host of brethren peeping out fearfully from behind him in the archway. He stood as upright as his years allowed, leaning upon his tall staff, crooked into the traditional coiling serpents at its crown, carved and gilded and coloured with bright wings and flames.

A fierce exultation ran through the troops, scrambling to their feet, drawing weapons without orders. Here was food for slaughter upon a miserable stinking winter night; the sergeants held them back with low growling commands. The commander stood square in front of the gate, arms folded.

'You have now heard the rightful request of your lord and master. Deliver to me the Gift that Cannot be Refused, or this rat warren will be demolished.'

The abbot blinked rain out of his eyes, briefly considering whether or not rats congregated in warrens, and what volume of natural history might be consulted to verify this term. He then thought of many things that men might find hard to refuse.

'We have much gold here . . . take all you want.'

'I refuse your gold . . . it is forfeit in any case.'

'We have the wisdom of countless centuries inscribed within our library . . . secrets that no living man has ever seen.'

'I despise your puerile sentiment that poses as wisdom . . . all your fine vellums shall be burned, or turned into gloves and barrel bungs.'

The abbot was deeply shocked by this last suggestion, but not surprised. He paused for a moment as if in thought and replied: 'In my private chamber there is a deep wall cupboard with a hidden door and lock. In that cupboard is a tiny chest, and in the chest are three pills compounded of a substance that will lengthen the span of human life by . . . '

'I spit upon your charlatan claims, your pills, your potions, your superstitious rubbish!'

'Very well, since it is clear that you will refuse all lesser gifts, no matter how much they may benefit you, I now freely offer you that which no man can refuse . . .' As he spoke the abbot straightened his back, and the brethren drew back from him, leaving him standing alone in the gateway. The commander leaned forward, avid for his triumph. The abbot spoke in a quiet voice.

'Our payment is as it has always been from the beginning, and it is thus: *the bell that cannot be rung, the song that cannot be sung, and the book that cannot be written.* Take them freely, my son, and go in peace.'

As the abbot uttered these curious words, the rain stopped. The soldiers stood with jaws agape, the horses were silent, ears pricking up. The wind ceased to blow, and the moon appeared from behind the last rain cloud. She shone full into the face of the commander. His eyes rolled, his skin appeared mottled red, his mouth worked and his tongue slithered. A tiny roll of spittle oozed down his jaw. Tilting towards the abbot, he tried to lift a hand, but it curled and dropped downwards, while with a sudden staggering motion he fell over, striking his head against the gatepost.

In that terrible silent moment, the abbot stepped back into the gateway, and the steward closed and barred the gate. The soldiers looked foolishly at one another, cleared their throats, spat and coughed. Some began to drift off quietly into the moonlit trees, leaving their pikes behind. The sergeants muttered together for a few moments, then began to pick up the discarded weapons and load them onto horses . . . they did not pursue the men, or issue any orders. No one touched the body lying by the gate, and one by one the abbey lights went out as a bell tolled softly high in the tower.

SEQUANA
THE SACRED DUCK

Firstly, for those who are not familiar with the archaeology of pagan Europe, the origin of 'Sequana'. Dedications to this goddess, dating from the Romano-Celtic first century BC, and votive ducks, have been found at or near to the source of the River Seine in France.[17] Indeed, *Sequana* and *Seine* are likely to be etmyologically related. But fact is less important in this humorous tale than fable; this is, on one level, a fable concerning society, expansion, and seemingly inevitable war. Upon a deeper level it concerns the folly of attempting to provide for all eventualities; the insurance syndrome or capitalism gone mad. But in its deepest level, it is a *ludibrium* or silly tale about the creation of the world, from its primal appearance as a theriomorphic duck goddess, inside her egg-like white enclosure, to the proliferation of energies and entities that inevitably manifest around her sacred presence. And at the end of it all, as in all creation tales, even the goddess herself bows to the mysterious powers of dissolution.

The Four Sacred Directions and the expansion of interlinked sequences from a central locus are featured in this tale, and certain images, such as the procession of hounds and warriors are found in the illuminations to early gospels such as *The Book of Kells*. Convoluted patterns were a feature of Celtic art, but they may be traced back through their maze-like connections to very simple fundamentals.

Fables, often employing animals as the main protagonists, formed an important part of oral tradition, and were once part of nursery education or family entertainment. We might add, only slightly in jest, that such tales may link back to ancient magical traditions of totem beasts, in which specific creatures represent energies of places, gods and goddesses, or phases of universal, planetary, or regional creation and dissolution. They also represent energies and psychic constructs or entities within ourselves, and the fusion of the inner totem animal with the magical image of that same animal is a major magical achievement.

We find such totem beasts in world mythology and many religious

traditions, but their enabling and empowering functions have generally been forgotten in all but the primal or chthonic magical arts. Part of the modern revival of magic as a means of changing awareness and transforming the individual is concerned with the redevelopment of totem beasts as a valid means of working.[1]

But I accept no responsibility for those who seek Sequana the Sacred Duck as their totem beast, even though she has certain good qualities, such as quietly minding her own business, and recognizing the inevitable when it finally approaches her nest.

SEQUANA THE SACRED DUCK

(Or: How the king of the North came to invade the South)

In the gloom-enshrouded forests of the North, where ancestral spirits dwell among great trees while kings and heroes die of uttermost boredom during long bleak winters, was one of the Three Curious Households of Britain. The king of those regions had been given a gift by his cousin in distant Gaul; this gift was nothing less than a living incarnation of a goddess. The goddess was Sequana, she who ruled a long river in Gaul, worshipped by a people renowned throughout civilization for their poor drainage. She took the physical form of a sacred duck.

From before the dawning of the first sun it had been decreed by the power that made the gods that Sequana the Sacred Duck should live according to mystical laws. The laws were thus: she must dwell within a small enclosure of ellipsoid shape, coloured perfectly white, with a wall of exactly five hand-spans height set about it. So such an enclosure was built by the men of the North for the goddess, the sacred duck spent her time within it happily, and all was well.

During a particularly hard winter the primary wise bard observed aloud that a wall of five hand-spans height was not tall enough to keep out the wolf, the fox, or even the rabbit. So the king of the North brushed the frost from his beard and decreed thus: two hounds would be set to guard Sequana the Sacred Duck. So two hounds were trained and set to guard, a light-coloured hound with black-tipped ears to be alert during the day, and a dark-coloured hound with fawn-tipped ears to watch through the night. These hounds paced around the enclosure of Sequana the Sacred Duck, which was just large enough for two hounds to encircle nose to tail, which event occurred at dawn and dusk of each day as they exchanged guard duty. During the summer the light-coloured hound paced for longer than the dark one, and during the winter the dark-coloured hound slept less than the light one. Thus their labours were evenly divided through the year, and all was well.

The primary wise bard observed aloud one day that if the height of the enclosure was low enough to admit the ravening wolf, fox, and rabbit, then it might also admit a hound . . . no matter how well-trained that hound might be. So the king of the North appointed two spearsmen, one fair-haired to watch the night hound, and one dark-haired to watch the day hound. Thus the men guarded the hounds, the hounds guarded the enclosure, and the enclosure guarded Sequana the Sacred Duck. She was coloured black and white, with rainbow-hued wing feathers, and a bright red face. While she remained in the enclosure, all would be well.

It soon became clear to the more observant men of the North, who could see beyond their steaming breath through the frost, that this collection of men and hounds would need food over and above the usual quantity. Did they not spend much time outdoors, during the cold wet of summer and the freezing snow of winter? So the primary bard shrewdly pointed out to the king that on a black night filled with shivering fog even a trained warrior might be sorely tempted to eat a sacred duck.

The king grandly decreed that four speckled red and black cows would be kept in an enclosure of withies, which would run in a circle around the ellipse that was around Sequana the Sacred Duck. So every full moon a cow was slaughtered to feed the men and hounds. In the many days when the moon could not be seen through the snow clouds, time was calculated by an assistant bard, who also counted the number of replacement cattle from the royal herd. For several months all was well, but the men who guarded the hounds who guarded the enclosure of five handspans height complained that they were warriors, and not cowherds. So the king, wiping condensation from his nose and eyebrows before it could freeze, appointed an ugly, bad tempered, warty, slouching fellow to herd the cows. For a while, all was well, and the assistant bard counted the moons and the cattle.

The primary wise bard soon observed aloud that it was against the laws of the Great Goddess for three men (or to be precise two men and a male cowherd) and two hounds to be without females of their own kind. It might also be better to have a bull in with the cows that they might breed, rather than replace those eaten from royal stock every month. The king gave this matter deep thought while shivering in his sweat-lodge. Upon seeing the day and night hounds attempting to engage in fruitless all-male coupling when they met nose to tail at dawn and dusk, he decreed that all members of the household of Sequana the Sacred Duck should have mates according to their own kind. So it became known as one of the Three Curious Households of Britain, for it hatched from a duck egg.

The two guards chose two large-breasted curly haired girls who were used to sleeping out in the woods and fields; the two hounds were mated with two brindle bitches; and the four speckled cows were blessed with a huge white bull with red ears and spreading long horns decorated with golden tassels and silver bells. The warty cowherd sneaked away one night to return with the largest, ugliest, worst-tempered woman that had ever been seen in the kingdom of the North before or since, and that in a land famous for its bad-tempered women!

In the middle of her perfectly white enclosure Sequana the Sacred Duck took no mate; she was content, being the incarnation of a goddess and dedicated to a higher fate. The king sent the primary wise bard to Brittany to pursue advanced magical arts, and for a while there was peace, and all went well.

So it was that one wet grey dawn in midsummer, the king of the North arose and walked out with his attendants and his court. He walked to the top of a thickly-wooded hill upon which no man might stand unless he was in the company of a king, and then only in high midsummer. This hill overlooked the valley of the Household of Sequana the Sacred Duck, and when the king peered through the mists, and when the hail-spattering winds blowing from all directions at once had parted these mists for his kingly benefit, this is what he saw.

First there was a black and white duck with irridescent plumage sitting within a small, bright, irregular enclosure. Around this enclosure was a large pack of hounds milling in all directions, some black, some white, some mottled. They ran and crouched and leapt yelping and copulating without cease or hindrance; young, healthy, glossy hounds, old grey muzzled hounds, and little wriggling squealing puppy-dogs.

Next there was a company of men holding spears; they stood in a firm square, shoulder to shoulder about the hound pack, allowing the animals a measured space in which to disport themselves. These warriors stood alternatively dark-haired and light-haired, while at the corners of the square formation were those with red hair. They numbered many hundreds, and regularly broke the square formation to march up and down with praiseworthy discipline, ever maintaining the measured space that held the pack of hounds, and soon returning to a square again. Beyond these warriors was a woven circular enclosure of withies, with both an inner and outer wall, making a double ring. This enclosure was so vast that the outermost wall could hardly be seen, so far away was it built around the edges of the great valley that held the Curious Household.

Within the great enclosure of woven withies was a herd of cattle more numerous than the stars of the sky, more tempestuous than the storm-wrenched waves that guard distant Ireland. The bulls bellowed and trampled to shake the earth from sleep, the cows stood with udders bursting warm milk for the bawling, suckling calves, and a throng of warty, ugly, screaming brats ran in and out among the cattle, herding them aimlessly with pointed sticks.

Also within the great enclosure the king saw a huge camp of untanned cattle-hide tents, sheltering many full-breasted pregnant women, with children too young to be guards or cattle herds. One immense ugly fellow lay fast asleep, while his hideous wife poured abuse and scorn and insults into his right ear without pausing for breath. Great iron cauldrons had been set up, and the smoke of dung fires and the smell of boiling beef wafted to the royal nostrils as the king stood upon that hill on midsummer's day.

The king of the North stood silent awhile in the refreshing rain. Indeed, nothing that he might have said could have been heard by his attendants or his court, so great was the bellowing, screaming, thundering of hooves, clashing of spears, tramp of marching feet and frenzied barking and yelping. Waving his arms in a kingly manner, he led his company back to the royal dwellings, where a faint rumbling could still be heard through the thick stone walls.

'Send for the primary bard out of Brittany' was what the king finally said, and no other word did he utter all that year until the bard returned at midwinter.

But the primary wise bard was shrewd and observant. He guessed that all was not well when he travelled through the land and felt the earth trembling, and when he neared the royal domain and saw trees toppling to make cooking fires, tent poles, and spears for the growing host of the Household of Sequana the Sacred Duck. So when the bard entered the royal presence, he flung himself down in the flat submissive posture of a mere supplicant, and said loudly to the dirty floor, 'Great king, we have the men, we have the arms, we have the supplies. Your idea to invade the South is clearly inspired by your divine ancestors and will undoubtedly be character-forming for the nation.'

So the king forgave the bard, and had the great war horns blown. For ten days that host passed through the borders, leaving not a blade of grass growing, not a tree unfelled, not a river undried. Wherever they passed there were mountains of beef bones, old shoes, soiled napkins and dogs' excrement.

Back in her peaceful enclosure in the heart of an empty bare valley, where even ancestral spirits had no dwelling place, Sequana the Sacred Duck opened one bright yellow eye and looked South. This is what she saw:

A wall of perfect whiteness only five hand-spans high, and the tail end of a rabbit suddenly leaping away off that wall. The sight of this creature raised certain questions in her normally placid mind, and so she opened her other eye, the blue one, to look North. This is what she saw:

The other half of that perfectly white ellipse of wall, and over the top of the wall two sharp pointed red ears rising. These ears ascended towards the gathering storm clouds, propelled upwards by a red mask face with huge compelling eyes, a long tooth-filled snout and a wet lolling tongue. This terrible face drew after it a neck with a red and white ruff and two shoulders upon lean legs and two long, fine pointed paws with black claws of perfect shining cleanliness, marred only by a little snow and dried blood.

So it was that in the land of the North, within a great valley, within a double circling enclosure of woven withies, within a white enclosure of five hand-spans height, Sequana the Sacred Duck bowed her neck to the inevitable unopposed fox.

THE YOUTH

One of the most interesting and least discussed aspects of meditation or magical work is the continual access to alternative myths, gospels, teachings, and schools of inner development. On one hand such ramblings are dismissed as trivial nonsense, and in most cases this is probably an accurate summary. On the other hand, we find pompous allusions to great 'secret teachings' 'initiate's books' and the like. Such claims, even when the material is of value, are surely dangerous and potentially corrupting, for they lead to false notions of superiority.

This short tale is an extract from one of the alternative gospels, books, myths, or schools of inner teaching. In the mythology of our own world, a Celtic variant called *The Mabinogion* deals with a cycle of adventures woven around one *Mabon*, whose name simply means son. In Welsh legend and Romano-Celtic inscriptions he appears as Mabon, Son of Modron; or Son, Son of Mother. Thus he is part of the world-wide myth of the Great Mother and the Son of Light. In the story of 'The Gift that Cannot be Refused' (page 47) we touched upon another alternative gospel or sacred tale, in which the spiritual child is a girl. That variant hardly ever seems to arise in our world, though there is ample historical, poetic and mythical evidence that it may have been suppressed. This suppression is explored in the satire 'The Dream of Saint Austin' (page 107).

Visualization

More specifically 'The Youth' deals with the Four Implements and Four Elements, as shown in our Figure One (page 48). One method of examining any myth or magical tale is to consider it in the context of such a master glyph, but it must be stressed that mere intellectual correspondences are only a minor process, and that most of the work is undertaken through meditation and visualizing on levels that transcend or underpin superficial mentation.

Tarot images and patterns

As a visualizing aid, this story could be used with the tarot trumps of The Fool, the Four Aces, and Judgement from *The Merlin Tarot* or any tarot deck that attunes to esoteric tradition. An interesting and productive exercise is to take this tale, and its six images, and to seek out the further tales implied within it by drawing further cards. These further images will lead on from where this tale ends, or may open out as hidden or embedded episodes between each phase of the major fourfold pattern of the main narrative.

THE YOUTH

Many tales are told of the Blessed Youth and of his travels. Some are written into great books bound with hides of creatures long extinct, coloured with brilliant letters, each letter being both a picture and a story in itself. Some are set into the hearts of rough crystals awaiting their moment of future speech; others are more simply kept in the timeless memories of ordinary people. Such tales are handed down from mother to daughter, seeded in dream time, percolating through the centuries as gold seeps through the veins of rock.

And there is another source for such magical enduring tales . . . the well-spring of vision that floods the waking mind suddenly with light. In that light images are seen, not mere pictures, but emblems of such vitality and joy that each instant bursts forth into time containing within itself hours or even years of telling and retelling. It was in this manner, we are told, that the Blessed Youth himself saw certain possible futures, drew occasional obscure guidance upon his quest.

Some such visions remain as songs or riddles, other come as dreams, familiar yet instantly forgotten upon awakening. A few are still carved upon ancient buildings or into worship stones hidden in open windy places. One such tale was long preserved in the ancient houses of power and service, those confluences of time, space and energy known in our world as temples or abbeys. Fragments of this one tale are found in heretical gospels, prophetic books, picture cards, and fireside entertainments. Listen now, if you have ears to hear, to the story of the Blessed Youth and his vision of The Weaver.

During one of his many wanderings, the Youth crossed over a

great plain, barren and waterless. He carried only a staff, a small water flask, a leather bag containing bread, a small round targe or shield, and a long sharp knife. There was nothing alive to hunt, nothing growing to harvest, and little enough to see but the endless dry earth and ceaseless sun by day. Each night he would sleep in the chill, under strange stars, marking the direction of that one constellation still familiar to him. Those Seven Sisters led him, in time, to another place . . . which is told of in another tale.

On his third night of travelling across the plain, the Youth fell into a strange lethargy too vague to be called despair, too wakeful to be called sleep, too drowsy to be fully aware. As he slipped into the half-world, the dream-world, in this enfeebled fashion, he rolled over onto his left side. His knife became caught in the hollow behind his knee, and the pressure of movement made it twitch upwards, giving him a most painful cut in the genitals from the tip of its unsheathed blade.

Coming suddenly awake, the Youth leapt up and trod violently upon one end of his staff, which sallied into the air and landed him a hard knock upon his forehead. This bitter blow left a mark upon his brow that was to remain with him for the rest of his life, shining brightly in moments of inspiration or terror. Not being able, as it were, to hold both foundation and crown at once, he tottered about for a few seconds, flailing his hands and arms up and down between his two agonized extremities. In so doing, he stood suddenly upon his round targe or shield, which instantly flew out from under him, as such objects will. Shooting forcefully from his unsteady feet, it caused him to fall flat upon his back on the hard bitter earth.

Between the time of slipping and the time of landing painfully upon the ground, the Blessed Youth endured a most curious vision, which widened out like a strong door opening at last upon a hidden world. His glimpse within that world lasted for a period of time in which you or I might have been born, lived, died and carried back to rebirth no less than thirty-three times. Yet within an instant he was flat upon his back groaning with pain and regretting the day that he had dared to sneak away from home.

During the first part of his fall, as the targe slipped out so cunningly from under his feet, as he began to topple gracelessly to the ground, passing from vertical to diagonal, this is what he saw:

A door, and upon and before and yet within and part of that door, a silver man with two heads looking both outwards and inwards. This silver man opened the door, which is to say that he turned his inward-looking head outwards and his outward-looking head inwards . . . and so the world within and beyond was revealed.

During the second part of his fall, as the feet of the Blessed Youth left the ground altogether for the merest instant and his flailing body passed from diagonal to horizonal, this is what he saw:

Beyond the door was a moving coloured cloud seething and turning in all directions. It seemed to part and move both away and towards itself; the colour of this cloud was white and pearl and purple and it drew his eyes exactly as a serpent draws jewels inevitably from the rock. The cloud first thickened then thinned, moving in two spiralling directions, dissolving into a scattering of white and rainbow lights upon utter blackness. Each light left a trail of living colours that endured for both time and no time. Each of the spiral directions resolved into points, and each point glowed until it assumed an individual colour, joined by a thread to all other lights, interlinked and alive as one community, one congregation.

During the third and last part of his fall, the Blessed Youth transited most rapidly the short space between air and earth. Finally he gained a perfect horizontal position for the length of one agonized indrawn breath, and in that moment, this is what he saw:

Beyond the web of stars, within utter blackness, a shape assumed form. Immense beyond all concept of size, this shape became the figure of a woman. As it resolved it seemed to both shrink and grow, until the woman was clear to see and of human proportion, yet more vast than the space within which she sat. All love and terror were in that dark form, her hands moved in a blur across a ball of threads hovering before her where she sat. From this ball lines were cast off into the void, each spiralling to carry the lifetime of a star . . . its utterance forth from nothing, its dance across time and space, and its final leap into the void unknown drawing away all attendant worlds, all dependent life.

Even as her hands moved ceaselessly upon the spinning ball between two looms hidden in darkest shadow, she began to turn her face towards the Youth. As she turned her form began to pulse with light, and in that turning and upsurge of brightness, he endured an agony such as may not be told, for no mere words can touch upon its truth.

Just as it seemed that the Youth might look full upon the face of the Weaver, his agony turned about itself and became ecstasy. In that moment his body was flushed and roused with an inner fire, then washed and cooled by dark waters rushing into emptiness between the spiralling stars.

Now the fall of the Blessed Youth had ended, and the back of his head banged hard against a rock, rolling to one side and hitting his water flask. The stopper of the flask was knocked out by the force of the blow, and the precious water poured across his face, waking him instantly from unconsciousness. Now he was out in the desert without water, with the sun about to rise. He felt his hand wrapped around something soft and yielding, and with his blurred vision saw that he clutched the remains of his supply of bread.

So his vision ended and grounded. What and who he met with the rising sun is for another tale, another pattern.

THE SONG OF SMALLNESS

Several of the stories in this collection are derived from or expanded out of songs. Some, such as the Legend of the Horses, embedded within the story 'Fives', page 93, or that of Tam Lin, found in 'The Game of Chess', page 157, are based upon oral tradition. Others, and the present story is one, come from new songs. The process is, perhaps, worth describing carefully, as it is very different to the sweat and toil of creative writing as it is normally understood and experienced.

Firstly the song is born complete in the consciousness: not line by line or note by note, but complete, like an explosion, a sunburst, a potency opening out. Words, music, and visionary images all appear simultaneously. This concentrated in-burst is then written out into our usual language, and defined upon a musical instrument.

As a long-time professional writer, song-writer and composer, I feel that these songs are very different from those that I might create for say, a play, a film, or for general song-writing in entertainment. They are, in short, *magical songs*. Rightly or wrongly, I feel that they come, fresh and living, from the same inner traditions and emblems that empower the ancient magical ballads or magical lyric songs found in folk tradition.

This particular song comes, geomantically, from a real location, and persisted in my mind for over a year until I finally brought it out into music. The story, however, unfolded much later. So we have a creation or tale-telling process of expansion: the germ of the song; its mani-festation as words and music; and a story within which the original song (originator of the tale) is embedded.

For those who like to explore themes, motifs and parallels, the tale is based, in part, upon the world-wide tradition of people who step entirely into other planes of existence. Every year thousands of people vanish. This is a documented fact in our information-obsessed culture; for centuries there have been stories concerning those who vanish into other dimensions, fairyland, strange worlds, mysterious realms. Many of the primal initiatory or magical arts are based firmly upon

contact with such worlds or dimensions, and upon being able to enter into them. There is an enduring tradition in Scotland, as in other parts of Europe, concerning people who vanish into fairyland and meet with the inhabitants therein. [18] This is supposed to have happened to certain historical persons, such as the thirteenth-century poet Thomas the Rhymer, and the seventeenth-century clergyman Robert Kirk.

Of course, there are other ways to interpret this tale, such as the seeming conflict between the inner life of the imagination and the outer life of daily work and duty, but we need not indulge in too many rational explanations. 'The Song of Smallness', both the tale and its originating song, also contains a number of what might be termed magical technicalities or rules and methods of working magic; I leave it to the reader to ferret these out.

THE SONG OF SMALLNESS

Every evening she would listen for the voice, just as light and darkness merged together. At first there would be a spattering of rain upon window glass, then a gust of wind through the susurrating poplars. If she listened too hard the sound would be lost amid her straining; but in the slap of the stream beyond the garden, the last call of evening birds, she knew that the voice was singing. Singing to her.

Inside the house was a bright warmth of lamps, heat from the stove, a kettle that bubbled and gurgled occasionally. All the toys and blue plates of small ambition, human levels too low for her wild outreaching. When she had first come here she had wanted to smash the glass, stamp upon the crocks, hurl the heavy pans out of their smug hanging places over the stove. In time her violence had faded, urged inwards towards a more potent centre of discontent. Indeed, she kept the house immaculate, as if the height of her despising lay in pretence of acceptance.

One evening as spring rain poured unceasingly, she sat in an upstairs room, watching light change over the water meadows. As clear, long, grey light clarified the trees, she heard the voice. First the drops of heavy rainfall ceasing, then a whisper among branches far away. It seemed as if the voice was suddenly close, yet more distant than the clouds.

'Small am I beneath your window,
Small am I hear me sing,
While you watch some distant road turning,
Oh the wind and rain.'

These words were woven into a high deep melody that swooped and fell, a leaf sliding through her mind at sunset. Instantly it was over, but she sat waiting and watching until total darkness surrounded the house.

Weeks passed before it came again, weeks of daily cleaning, cooking, tending. Caring without caring. She would find herself listening, hardly remembering what for, then suddenly resume her task, her pose. One evening while alone in the warm house, she heard it sing again. A water bird croaked across a dark river, a bat flew beyond the glass of the window, wind slid through the loose frame to stroke her cheek.

'Voice of bird-song, touch of leaf fall,
Small am I, hear me sing,
While you tend the mill of earth call,
Oh the wind and rain.'

Days became less tolerable after this second visitation. She became brighter and more cheerful, more neighbourly than ever. People commented on how she had come out of herself. But she had never, in truth, been so far within as she was at that time. Faces, voices, plans, hopes, flurried past her, meaningless phantoms of dream people. Hands held, plates clashed, forks and knives washed and wiped. Outer time seemed to accelerate to headlong speed; sunup and sunset merged into one hot glow, all false division melted through. The dream people, those who lived out of themselves, did not see this.

Each evening she would go into the upper room and watch for the long clear light that could be felt even under cloud shadows. waiting for the song to continue.

'Light my hand upon your forehead,
Small am I hear me sing,
While you lie still in your shadow bed,
Oh the wind and rain.'

By summer the haunting light came late. She took long walks alone in the meadows; cows bellowed, ducks laughed, green and gold life breathed upon her. The poplars danced full-leaved endless rhythms of a distant sea, and she would return to the house by sunset. Not once did she stay out in the open for the voice, it was as if she knew that it could come to her only through a veil. Human window glass, ephemeral stone walls. No direct contact was possible at that time.

By autumn, as the first grain was harvesting, she heard another verse:

'While the Moon turns, while the Stars crawl,
Small am I hear me sing,
Down the threads within the Lady's shawl,
Oh the wind and rain.'

Now the season drew in towards short daylight. There was less time to see off the games, shams, toys of daily life before her evening ritual of listening and waiting. None of the dream people seem concerned to disturb her window-sitting, so out of time and place that it hardly seemed to happen. They could not see it.

The leaves blew in great clouds and swirls across the river full of heavy brown water. Pools grew in the meadow, long trails of birds had flown to other lands. She longed now for another verse, feeling that the song was almost complete. The last verse, she knew, would arrive when the last leaf had fallen or the first ice skin wrinkled across the pools.

In the house the stove burned constantly. Thick stone walls grew warm slowly, buttresses against the coming force of cold. The last verse came very late, as stars burst out of the blue-black sky. Her breadth made mist upon the glass as she leaned forward to listen:

'Small am I to gain all openings,
Small am I, hear me sing,
In full time and tide I touch all things,
Oh the wind and rain . . .'

By morning a thick dense snow had fallen, with clouds driving up out of the East suddenly. All shapes upon the ground were levelled into a smooth white mirror for the hard day. As the first distant shouts and laughter of children pulling sledges echoed across the water, a few of the dream people came up from the kitchen. They looked into her room, wondering where she might be.

THE WOMAN OF THE BIRDS SINGS A SONG

This tale, like 'The Song of Smallness' has a magical song embedded within it. I have briefly described the appearance of such songs within the imagination on page 73, but in this present context, which is an extract from a much longer narrative, I should say that the song came first. Indeed, I had written out the song and recorded it before the detailed visionary experience which led to the narrative itself, yet I am certain that the song was a first concentrated insight through a window of vision into another time or world. That window is described in the introduction to a second story telling of the same world, 'Touching the River' on page 85.

The song embedded within this tale is, essentially, a vision of a primal god of light, not light in a grand or metaphysical sense such as is found in state religion or even in true mysticism, but the potent light of the hearth, the first fire, the lamp that burns at midwinter. This is the first and last meaning of the sanctuary lamp found in churches and temples throughout the world, the little flame that brings radiance from one world to another.

Hence The Woman of the Birds, a matriarch who sees her tribe in and out of life and death, sings the Sleeping Song, a lullaby which holds a vision of the primal guardian god of light as a spell bringing peace and security.

THE WOMAN OF THE BIRDS
SINGS A SONG

Through the thick wood-smoke, she heard the faint crying of a child. The heavy woollen curtain fell closed behind her, and the sound became muffled, then the crying ceased. Ah well, they sometimes awoke again after the song.

Her thin hair was tugged and blown as with a sudden change of

wind the smoke blew free and she could look up at the stars. Already the autumn was close upon them, with a meagre harvest and the threat of an early hard winter. She wrapped her cloak close around her, and waved to the waiting women, who stepped forward to attend.

'A good healthy girl child. We are fortunate indeed.' But her thoughts were of a very different nature as they led her carefully through the wet, cold mud. Another mouth, another life to sing, and even though they were so few, food would be hard to save, hard to find. It was as if the land itself, the beloved land, turned against them all now, and no one knew how to set matters right. Her great store of songs offered nothing to appease the land, to still the bitter wind, to dry up the rain.

The next hut was dark. There was no smoke flying from its vent. Again, as was the custom, her women stepped aside and left her to enter alone. The crude wooden door scraped open, rasping until she winced with the hard screaming sound of it. Within was shadow, and a dim feeble light from a little lamp. Peering about she could just see the heavy crude beams of the low roof, and the earth of the dug-out floor was damp in her nostrils, the odour of long-time damp and no fire. Lit by the greasy flickering flame was a low bed of lashed poles and ferns. The figure upon the bed was still, wrapped in a dark fur. She knew only that it was an old man, one of the old Runners, they had said. He certainly would not run now.

She was almost reluctant to move towards that bed . . . as if it might be one of her old lovers from summer, long ago, lying with his back to her. She knew that this was nonsense, for her summer was so long past that she had outlived them all, each and every one. Perhaps that is where I have gone wrong, she thought, perhaps I am too old, too weak to sing the right songs. Perhaps the land cannot withstand my weakness. She snatched her thoughts tight, and quickly stepped across the chamber to sit upon a stool beside the bed. There she waited, quiet and half-sleeping in the cold and damp, waiting for him to speak or move. There was no urgency for this one, nothing to be saved or healed.

'Is that you, Mother of Song?'

'And who else would it be, Runner of Roads, to enter your own house unasked and without a gift for you?'

'Ah, but you do me honour. There are none left to bring me gifts now. All my family died long ago. Ach, but there is only me left, out of all that lovely crowd . . .'

'Then you and I, Runner, have something we already share. My own family is long gone with yours.'

He was shocked at this personal revelation, even through his great weakness. It was most odd for the Woman of the Birds to reveal her personal life. She was supposed to console him, hear his words, help him die. He did not want her memories, he wanted a song. But in that clarity that sometimes comes before a death, he suddenly realized how lonely she too must be, and from the musty fur stretched out his withered hand.

'Forgive me, Mother of Song, for my selfishness.' She touched the offered hand, and then held it gently in her own. Two frail weightless hands together in the dark. So they sat awhile, each drifting slowly away, she to her memories and he to his gripping disease. A sudden sharp cough, followed by a heaving chest and painful spitting and slobbering brought him back from empty dreams to pain.

'Ach, Mother, it is death that you are holding the hand of. Please . . .' His words were smothered in the cough and the wheezing that wracked up out of his chest. Though tears squeezed out from her closed eyes, she waited on in silence. Ah but she had seen a great deal of death, and not only in this bad year. Somehow she was losing control of this particular death. This one old man, hardly known to her among the families that she sang for, touched her heart, even as a mirror of herself. And she was the one who had sung away so many without a qualm, pacified and rendered impersonal by the power of the rituals of her calling and her art and her ruling. She waited on.

'Mother of Songs,' came the long-expected whisper, 'She who enters a house giftless . . .' So now he remembered the ritual formula, now he was ready.

'She hears you, Runner of Roads.'

'As is my right, I claim the gift of song.'

'Whoever asks shall hear my song, whoever does not ask shall not hear.' And even as she intoned these long familiar words of power, she considered how well he remembered his part. Some were so far gone that she had to call in a woman to speak their part for them, but not him. He was a good boy, she thought, holding his aged mottled hand, a good boy.

'Oh Mother, there is no fire . . .' His voice was faint, almost lilting like a child. She had awaited another formal line of ritual, and for an instant did not grasp his words.

'Yes, well perhaps it has gone out this while past.'

'No, no, the song. That is the song, Mother, that is to be my gift.' Puzzled, she knew that she was somehow failing him. The cold air filled with the smell of blood, and with it mingled a sweet sickly odour that made her dizzy and disgusted. Suddenly she knew what he was asking for. She could not see his face, or the clots of putrid blood upon the fur, but the touch of his hand had communicated a brief flickering image to her inner eye.

She saw a spiral of warm golden light tinged with rose red, and kneeling upon one knee within the centre of that spiral was a man. And what a man! His flowing bright hair swept about his beautiful strong face, and in his hand was a long carven rod. He knelt to tend the fire that illuminated his exquisite shape, and the light spiralled out from the fire and himself as one.

But I have only just sung that song, that very verse, she cried in her heart. Your own mother must have sung you that song before you ran your first race along the great wooden roads through the marshes. The hand within hers was growing cold, and it squeezed gently.

'The song, Mother of Songs . . . the gift.' And she had just left a new-born girl child with that same gift. There were powerful songs for dying, but this old man begged of her the song for baby-sleeping. She should not deny him his right, she knew. Then again she saw clearly the image of the young man tending the fire, and the rightness of the song flooded in upon her. It was indeed the song for this old one running away, he was a baby drifting into sleep, into the arms of She who bore him before his mother. The Woman of the Birds sniffed and cleared her throat, and in a pale wavering voice, steadily gaining strength, she sang:

'Now I sing you the song of sleeping,
The song that sends the sun to rest;
Once there was a time of crying,
Now that time is gone and past.
Hear the song, the song the swans sing
As they fly with their chains of gold,
Sleep, my love, while the secret stars swing
Over and over the turning world.

This is the song the song of the first one,
Who was the first to tend a fire,
Who guards the hearth from the chill and the night winds,
And sometimes shows you your heart's desire;

Like the waters that run on the sea sand,
Rest a moment between ebb and flow,
Lie at peace in the horn of the moon's hand,
Where the tide pulls
Only the morning will show . . .
Where the tide pulls
Only the morning will show.'

Not long after these last words were sung his hand fell out of hers. She reached for it, and her hand slithered across the matted wet fur robe lying upon his still body. When her women finally dared to come in, distraught with waiting, the lamp had gone out. They had to feel through the dark to find where she sat.

TOUCHING THE RIVER

This story, and its companion (page 79) 'The Woman of the Birds Sings a Song' come from a novel, as yet unpublished. Although these stories form distinct parts of a long developing narrative, they have certain distinctly magical aspects, both in their origin, and as separate tales in their own right. The entire novel derives from a vision, or perhaps 'window' might be a more appropriate word, of a culture in another world or time. The time may be far indeed from our own, but the world is perhaps our own in the distant past, or very close to it. The discerning reader who knows the west of England will be able to find where the stories are located, though it took me several months to suddenly discover this for myself.

The insight or trans-sight leading to these tales came complete while I was snowed in one unusually harsh winter, and having come, remains open whenever I choose to look through it. What is seen therein is both beautiful and sad. In this tale, we discover an annual ceremony, connected to the sanctity of the land. So much for the scene itself, but the process of vision and recounting has a further role within magical tradition which is worth describing briefly as follows.

Much nonsense is written about 'astral records' and 'past lives', but it holds a grain of truth. One of the key experiences and abilities, usually erratic, that derives from the disciplines of meditation and visualization, is an apparent insight into past or parallel cultures, worlds, places, and times. I keep the definitions deliberately variable, for egocentric folly blossoms from assuming that what is seen is 'accurate' or 'authoritative'. In fact, the vision itself is valueless, and even more than valueless if the seer always attempts to relate it to his or herself in a falsely gratifying manner.

Esoteric tradition teaches that when such visions come, we may note them down, but their true value is derived from applying what we see to an organic or holistic vision of the magical tradition itself. In other words, certain episodes, personae, rituals, and highly significant events, will be seen in such visions. They relate specifically to the magical and spiritual tradition which the seer undertakes; they are

never mere tourism or random episodes. If we accept this traditional teaching, the story which follows, although developed deliberately as a narrative, embodies certain primitive forms of magical art, and somehow relates to modern magical, meditational and visualizing disciplines and arts.

On a more psychological or allegorical level, we could see the overall setting of both stories, and of the entire novel, as a parallel to our modern world. Both, for example, involve cultures and environments which are dying. Both are concerned with the eternal theme of the Waste Land, which is central to Arthurian tradition, but derives from an earlier religious belief that the land and humanity must be in a resonant harmonious relationship. Few themes could be more appropriate to the present day.

TOUCHING THE RIVER

In the high, hot summer sun many feather fans danced and waved wildly, brilliant blurs of colour. Each was mounted upon a long pole coloured with stripes of red, green and black; each pole top bore a firmly lashed cross-piece painted yellow; above each cross-piece was a wide disc of feathers rising to the sky. Through the year feathers had been gathered from every bird trapped, netted, arrowed, tamed, hatched, or coaxed into reach; from hedgerows and marsh ditches, from tree-tops and fox kills. they were sorted into matching, blending and contrasting colours, and set upon discs of stiffened flax, woven with fine fish bones to gain strength. The patterns emulated a bridge of light that arched over the sky after rainfall on a sunlit day; yet not a single feather was tinted or dyed, and as each fan became worn or tattered with years of use, it was carefully repaired in the Feather Room.

In this chamber, lit by roof hatches open to sun-rays reflected by polished bronze mirrors, or by many oil-lamps in winter, sat men whose lives were dedicated to sewing and matching and perfection. Cross-legged upon the bare hard floor through all seasons, they used tiny bone needles and probes to prick and weave, setting quills tightly into fabric. The brightest feathers had once been traded for fresh water, dried fish, sweet fruits, with travelling men from far over the Western sea, but could no longer be obtained, as their ships had ceased calling.

The pulse of deep heavy-skinned drums surrounded the waving fans, pounding an incessant threefold beat that roared across the marshes, shaking the earth, until all who were not yet dancing walked, talked and thought to the sacred rhythm. The dancers moved in two teams; one dressed all in white, one in black. They leapt and squatted like frogs, while some carried green branches and sprigs of white flowers. To the booming of the great drums they took turns to lead each other in the frog mating dance, now shuffling close to the earth, now leaping up croaking with outspread arms.

Leading this endless dance was a tall, tall being on thin stilt-legs. For this important role the smallest, lightest man was chosen, for he had to walk and even jump on stilts without rest or relief through the long summer day. He was wrapped in a loose grey robe of heron feathers, with a proud crested helmet upon his head. In his right hand he shook a rattle, a gilded skull holding tiny coloured stones locked within by crystal eyes. When he shook this flashing wonder, the dancers would fall flat upon the ground, moaning a low dirge. When he lowered it, when its face was partly hidden, they would leap up high and shout, and bright blaring horns would suddenly sound. Then the huge slow procession would move forward another few paces.

Sitting upon her Chair of Horns, the Woman of the Birds was carried upon the shoulders of a dozen squat muscular women. Each was dressed in thick leather armour, impressed with many swirls and images of running animals, flying birds, leaping fish. Each carried a bow with seven arrows and a short bronze sword, strapped cross-wise upon their breasts. These women wore masks upon their faces, looking rigidly ahead, and when they moved, achieved a strict marching unison. The secret of their unison pace lay in counting, an ability known to very few; during the greater part of the year these women, who had learned the arcane art from their mothers, worked hard as tally keepers in the communal storehouses. This, however, was their great and exclusive day of power.

The strain and weight of disciplined carrying in the hot sun made them sweat heavily, staining the leather black. To keep the air pure, nimble little boys darted about between the thick marching legs, waving clay pots on thongs, each pot smoking with aromatic gums and herbs smouldering upon willow charcoal. The masks worn by the women were coloured black and red, with white outlined eyes and full stiff beards of clayed wool. These masks were said to be very old, very potent, and so were only revealed for this one summer ceremony. At the close of the day, each mask had its name whispered, and was laid to sleep in a billowing bed of soft flowing cloth. The origin of the cloth was unknown, though some, greatly daring, said that it had been woven long ago in a single month from the webs of spiders. This shocking suggestion was seldom voiced loudly.

Along the raised causeway leading to the river, dust rose in thick dun clouds, covering the dancers from sight when the wind rested. Above the dust walked the stilted Heron, proud as a lordly bird of the marshes; he alone breathed freely, rattling his golden skull and making tiny leaps in ecstasy. Around the Woman of the Birds, upon her Chair, was a haze of dust, smoke, sweat, and incense. She could not hear the tramp of her bearers through the ceaseless roaring of the drum, but every measured rigid pace jolted her Chair, and so jarred her aching, aged bones. Once she had been proud and comfortable upon this annual ride to the river, but now it was a painful duty. Yet she sat calm and quiet, looking straight ahead, knowing that the entire people from the hill-fortress and her own marsh settlement were lining the causeway, watching not only the dancers, but herself, concealed and now revealed in the billowing dust and smoke.

The people swayed back and forth with arms linked, called and chanted to the Heron, drummers, trumpet and horn blowers, and stretched upon their toes or sat upon shoulders to see the Woman sitting upon her fabled Horn Chair. Whenever the long bronze trumpets and shrill animal horns blared, a sharp pain resonated above her left eye. She had learned to recognize and ignore it. It was a new pain among many familiar aches, but soon they would be at the river.

The crowd followed close behind the procession, dressed in their cleanest and best, waving branches, drinking heavily from skins and pots, munching little cakes, leaping, shouting, laughing, crying. Soon the procession would reach the three steps down to the water, and the people would be packed close together, intense, silent, hardly daring to breathe as the Woman descended from her Horn Chair.

Now, as six more joltings ceased and dancers mimed death, she looked up to see the hill-fort with its earthen and log walls rising bold and green against the sky and distant blue sea. Seldom had she seen it so from this distance, and she secretly blessed the tiny wind that had chosen to blow clean air and carry dust away from her face for this moment of clarity. The winter had been long and bitter, followed by a thaw of floods and drownings, with many animals rotting from the hooves where they stood and starved in the sodden pastures. Yet now the early summer threatened drought, and though she knew it was bad luck to think it, she feared another harsh winter beyond the dry summer. Ten steps forward, then another long wait before the roaring of voices and trumpets. Before next summer she must have firm words with the Heron . . . he rattled too often and leapt too little. They were both old.

As the booming and braying and rich scented air wove their spell, many of the faces in the crowd were transformed, showing blank empty eyes. A few dancers fell rolling and babbling in the dust; their families carried them carefully to one side, either to pour cold water over their heads or to furtively listen to their utterances. On recovering, each would return immediately into line, croaking, squatting, leaping, falling again.

Just upon the edge of her sight, the Woman saw a couple slipping off into the meadows still green from the water nearby. She should have scowled, but she smiled. Once she too had slipped away before the ritual touching of the river, and the result had been a fine strong son. Long dead.

Now the Horn Chair was lowered to the ground, and a great crescendo of drumming and screaming rasping horns mounted up to the sky, causing birds to rise from the distant inlets of the marsh, and men to stop up their ears, turn up their eyes whitely, and faint. The instant that her foot touched the earth, all sound ceased. A baby whimpered and was quickly muffled upon the mother's breast. Far away the Woman heard gulls calling in the bright sky, and it seemed that she could smell the sea. Unsupported, as was the way, she took the three steep irregular steps down to the river. It was running far below the lowest step, and she realized suddenly that she would have to stretch to reach the surface of the water. Loss of dignity at clambering down and stretching out did not concern her, but she wondered if she would be able to rise again unaided. It was forbidden to touch her until she had touched the river.

Carefully, painfully, she lowered herself and stretched out upon the dusty flower-strewn step; lying flat upon her stomach, she reached her withered arms to the water, to touch the slow-moving brown river.

How many times had she touched this water? Brown and slow as it was today, black and full and fast, green and gentle, it seemed to flow through her memory in many colours, each one for a year, a child, a lifetime, many lifetimes. The very tips of her old fingers touched the surface of the water, and she felt a shock, a strange power flow into her. It was like nothing she had experienced. Somehow, she knew, the river had changed since the last touching. It was traditional to rise, and bless the people, saying that the river was good and that the harvest would be better, but this strange touch and wild power had pushed the words right out of her mind . . . she who knew so many songs was suddenly unable to recall the most common verse of blessing. Finally she stood upright, turning to face the tense, breathless crowd. Were they aware of her shock? Had they seen her body jump and tremble? She opened her eyes and looked upon them; the man-women, the warriors, the workers, the feather weavers, the singers, the runners, the families. Then her memory returned, as if the energy that had suspended its normal flow had calmed or become absorbed. Raising both arms above her head she gasped out the ancient formula:

'River and sky are joined by land,
Rise and be blessed,
Be blessed with fruit and joy,
Be blessed with children and laughing,
Be blessed with peace and contentment.'

Only then did her women rush forward to help her onto the Horn Chair, and as the crowd went wild with screaming, laughing, tearing of hair and cutting of breast and forearms, they carried her back to the cool shadow of her quiet chamber at the back of the great Woman Hall.

FIVES

This tale derives from a story-cycle which I began in 1980, while snowed in to my house in the centre of Bath during an exceptionally severe winter. Some of the mythical elements in the tale, and in other stories in this collection associated with it (see 'The Fairy Harp', page 115) are derived freely from the ancient worship site of the hot springs of Aquae Sulis,[19] Bath, England, but they are certainly not Celtic or Roman, and are not to be taken too literally. The story contains many levels of paradox and cross-reference based upon myths, but as I have said previously, to attempt to decipher them all would be a waste of time and energy.

The second tale embedded within the main text is taken from an ancient traditional ballad, 'The Two Brothers', and its companion ballad 'Edward', at one time known and sung all over Britain, Ireland, Europe and America, and reputed to link back to a pagan matriarchal cult, perhaps at the roots of Celtic and pre-Celtic society. Such oral magical ballads and tales were preserved well into the twentieth century, and should not be thought of as obscure or isolated relics of early poetry; they were, and still are, part of a living collective tradition of narrative dramas and images.

The exotic details of this embedded tale, such as the blood-drinking horses, the mother at her loom weaving daylight, and the convoluted explanation of the plot given by the story-teller, are of course my own, though I should state that after I had visualized the story-teller sitting in his round chamber by a steaming vent underground, he told this embedded or interlaced story without any help or contrivance from me.

One of several promising visualizations within 'Fives' is to build the underground chamber as described, with the ancient man sitting upon the edge of the steaming well. He is a vast repository of entertaining, obscure and paradoxical tales, myths, riddles, jests and insults. The real problem is persuading him to stop talking, which, once he has started, is virtually impossible.

And what about 'Fives'? The verse at the opening of the tale gives

a complete key to the strange language spoken by Windfall, the main character, when he finally recovers his power of speech after a harrowing experience has rendered him temporarily silent. Cryptography has, historically, been associated with magic, not least in the person of Doctor John Dee, who gave the world the so-called Enochian language and alphabet, which he and his seer Edward Kelly transmitted from another world during the sixteenth century.

It should not be too hard for the diligent reader to solve the puzzle posed by the verse, which is partly cryptographic but couched in traditional magical terminology, with certain rules relating to the sanctity of letters. Having done so, you may read Windfall's immortal words for yourself. If you think that you have solved the cryptic language, please write to me care of the publishers, but I reserve the right of explanation in the time-honoured manner of bards, magicians, and smart alecks. Meanwhile, for those of you who are determined to solve the puzzle, I can only say, in words that might have been uttered by the old man, the story-teller within the tale, *Wmo wenya usupbt?*

FIVES

In fives I run against the sun
My spirit lost two children gone;
My tongue direct is now enchained
Five crossed the bridge
Yet five remained.

There was once an ignorant and innocent young man who accidentally murdered an old woman. Well, she provoked him into it by goading him and taunting him as she hung there, for she sought death. He being fairly stupid and armed with a spear, as he had been set to guard her, she being a malefactor, he stabbed her just as she had intended. She laughed as she died, and must have put a heavy curse upon him, for he could not speak a word from that moment onwards, but only croak like a palsied frog.

Anyway, the youth, who was called Windfall, ran away. Not because of the killing, you understand, but because his wise elders would have beaten him to a pulp for dereliction of duty. The old woman was supposed to hang upside-down for days until some information fell out of her, but Windfall had, in his stupidity, given her a quick and merciful death. His own life, thereafter, was not worth a flea.

If I were to tell you all of his adventures in one story we would be here for a long, long time, but it is the matter of 'Fives' that I am leading up to, so please be patient. While fleeing, Windfall fell in with two rather pleasant women, or so he thought. This mother and daughter took him in to their delightful, warm underground home, which was superior indeed to the cold mud and raw berries which had been his dwelling and sustenance before their meeting.

But, as is often the way with women, they merely sought to use his manly body for their own purposes. Knowing nothing of women or of sexual matters, Windfall drank freely of the honey wine that they offered him, and lolled back upon the deep furs that filled their underground home. It was not long before they sought him out in the warmth and dark, but as they closed in upon him his head cleared a little with the shock, fright, and confusion that rushed in to replace alcohol.

Determined to flee these groping, grasping women with their hot hands and strong white arms, rubbing stiff breasts and hungry seeking mouths, he jumped quickly to his feet. That is, he tried to jump, but the plenteous mead that had been so kindly given to him along with the roast meat and fresh bread would only let him stagger, fermenting ceaselessly.

During his drunken stagger in the dark, amid such cooing and rustling and slithering from two unseen women, Windfall put out both arms to steady himself, knowing that a firm friendly stone wall was close at hand. But where it should have been solid stone that met his touch and held his weight, it was, in fact, nothing. He fell forward, banging his head heavily upon a low arch or lintel; he then suffered a long grazing of his tender forehead, as if he collapsed within a diminishing hole or hollow in the chamber wall, which is exactly what it was, and crawling forward in pain, he soon found himself on his knees, barely able to squeeze ahead. This hardly worried him, despite the blood seeping into his eyes from his cut forehead, for he was only too relieved to discover that as soon as he was inside this tunnel, the questing noises of the ardent females were muffled then lost. How strangely they had fondled his body!

In this compressing tunnel, Windfall heard water running. He remembered that as he had downed his last flagon of mead before, as he had thought, a good night's rest, he had heard the flow of water seeming to merge with the subdued crackling of the fire in the hearth. He knew now that this mysterious sound had come from the hidden passage way in the wall; it must lead somewhere, and if he followed the water to its outflow, he would be back above ground again. This was, of course, totally spurious, fallacious, superficial, pseudo-logical and ill-considered on his part, but such was his essential nature at this time in his life.

Feeling his way through the damp darkness, unable to see, he could sense that the rock walls were both wet and warm. The hot springs of the swamp above, through which mother and daughter had led him after their meeting, could be felt seeping through the rocks here below. Suddenly the passage made a sure dive downwards, and Windfall could feel worn steep steps beneath him, as he groped forward on his hands and knees. Reasoning that he might slip and injure his head a second time, he turned himself about and climbed backwards, feeling each perilous damp step with his bare feet, and keeping his tense body close to the rock wall.

As a result of this reversed mode of progress it was some time before he realized that the passage way was growing lighter, and when he reached the end of the long flight of steps, he discovered that there was sufficient room to stand upright, and a dim orange light to see by. As he stretched, the first sight that he saw was a figure of a bear, carved into the mineral-encrusted roof above his head. The second sight that he saw was a passageway about the height of a man (or, he hardly dared to think, of a woman), leading on ahead, with light from some unseen source at its ending. The floor of this tunnel swirled with hot waters, yet Windfall strode forward, slushing through, determined to find a way out if such a way was to be found.

The light radiated from a narrow, tight arch at the end of the long tunnel, and as he approached this arch, he was unsure for some time about the true nature of what he saw. At first he took it to be two artificial trees carved into the rock, with their branches intertwined at the crown of the arch. Stepping closer, he revised his first opinion, and wondered if, in fact, these were not real trees, long-petrified by the flow of rich mineral water, for they were striated and infilled with blood-red, green, black and dark blue metallic mineral deposits.

When Windfall finally reached the arch, he realized that it was not built of tree at all, but of the likenesses of a man and woman linked together, leaning towards one another at the crown of the arch. Quite unused to such startling representations of human-ity, he studied these astonishing figures closely, comparing them to his own naked body, as he knew it, and the memory of the only naked woman he had ever seen (though not, after his recent experience, the only naked woman he had ever felt). This memory was, of course, that of the Old Woman Hung Up By Her Feet, whom he had killed only a few days before.

He concluded that, in every respect, the male figure carved into the rock before him corresponded generally to himself, while the female was much like the woman whom he stabbed to death, albeit younger, and with certain bulges reminiscent of those younger females who had but recently tried to have their way with him.

Clearly the habits of this land into which he had wandered were very different from his own, with women equal to men or even, terrible thought, superior, He wondered, greatly fearing, what his Elders would have made of mother and daughter in the underground chamber. It certainly would not have been easy to capture them and hang them up by their feet until they talked . . . and in any case they had hardly stopped talking at all, except between drink and mouthfuls of meat, which they took in turns, one speaking while the other swallowed or chewed. Oh, and of course they were briefly silent when, strangely, they had touched him on the mouth with their lips!

Trying to dismiss such thoughts from his mind, Windfall looked upon the rock figures before him. At the feet, or roots, of the male figure, was a bucket or cauldron, while the female figure held a long staff or spear. They merged together at the top of the archway, their heads joined side to side as one, two faces looking down at him with four blank eyes. From their twin mouth above the archway issued a fine spray of hot steam. Stepping through this invigorating and refreshing curtain, he felt the last curdling of mead and meat being cleansed from his brain.

He fell, of course. But it was only a short fall into yet another rounded rock chamber, quite unlike the one from which he had so recently fled. Lit by a large number of lamps near the roof, upheld by stone figures carved around and directly out of the walls, this chamber was bare but for two things. One was a huge vent in the floor from which issued puffs and blasts and belches of live steam, while the other was a man who sat upon the low wall that surrounded the vent.

Never had Windfall seen such an old man, or one so thin.

With long white flapping hair and a frail body that seemed ready to blow away in the blasts of steam, he stood up and came forward to meet his visitor. His walk was limping, but rapid and sure.

'Oh you really have made a right mess of it, haven't you . . .' he said without any formal introduction. 'A considerable knotted, gnarled and tangled mess, greasy and convoluted and disagreeable in the extreme. It will probably take you some long time and much redundant misplaced effort to set it aright. If you want my advice, as your undoubted spiritual elder and revered ancestor, you should have mounted them both. But you probably won't listen to me anyway. Well? Speak up boy, I don't have all night to wait for your feeble excuses. Why did you, or rather why *didn't* you do it?'

Astonished by this reception, and hardly comprehending what was said to him, Windfall opened his mouth and spewed out the first words that he had uttered since murdering Old Woman Hung Up By Her Feet.

'Wma ipo ti? Wmey an ymun rjafo? Mew du ipe kswa he?'

'Oho,' replied the elder, rubbing his nose, 'One question at a time, eh, my lad? I am, in a manner of speaking, your ancestor, though I sincerely hope that we are not actual blood relations.

'My present occupation is guarding this accursed well, which is no laughing matter I assure you. As for my knowing you, I could hardly avoid recognizing a fool who has utterly allowed himself to be flummoxed and coerced into following the wrong way at the wrong time into the wrong places. After all I did the same myself so often and for so long; until I eventually grew out of such bad habits. For habits are all that they are, mark by words. Stupidity is a habit, and not a condition. However no amount of mere *telling* will impress that truth upon you.'

'Gec I fos nuuk, I fos nuuk!' cried Windfall, half in joy and half confusion.

'Quite so, my boy, quite so. But you happen to be speaking in Fives. I can understand you perfectly well, of course, as I live in Fives most of the time anyway. But believe me when I advise you that it will do you no good whatsoever if you speak like that when you get out of here — if you ever do get out of here. It is quite likely that you will be locked up, if you get out, and exhibited for sport and derision. Perhaps you will just be stoned to a pulp by the first mob of innocent bystanders who happen to hear you speak.'

'Ac u exip iay? Wmoy un yma wet uoy? Yijj ho e gob ic tu!'

'Ah, well, the best way out of here is not at all the one that you
might think, or choose, or take. Sometimes you think that you
are out when you are not, or feel that you are in when you are
not really in at all. Why don't you stop prattling on, sit down,
and listen to a really good story?

'No, don't open your mouth to object, because it really is the
only way out for you. Show a little patience for once . . . if you
had only been patient with those lusty dames upstairs you
would not be in this pickle now. Or at least not in exactly the
same one, and although you will not believe me when I tell you
. . . you could have had a very pleasant time indeed up there, or
rather in there. I certainly did, though that was a very long time
ago and with different women. Or at least, I assume they were
different women. There we are, however, and here we sit. Now
listen closely to this story, and do not interrupt. If you do this
devious spring might rise up again and then you'll have to swim
for it. Listen well, for there are only a few left who could tell you
this story, and only a fool would pass up the opportunity to hear
and remember.'

Windfall was, as might be expected, amazed at such an out-
spoken elder, who seemed to know him so well. He sat obedi-
ently at the old man's feet, which were quite clean and pink and
wrinkled from the steam, presuming that he was about to learn
some complicated set of instructions for escape. He remained
silent, determined to benefit from the fruits of wisdom, though
his new-found tongue was twitching and itching, and his brain
was bursting with questions like maggots breeding in a sheep's
neck.

'Once upon a time', said the frail old man, breathing in steam,
'there were two brothers. They were two loving and handsome
brothers, as all brothers should be and many are not. One was
fair and golden as the summer sun on a bright summer morning,
while the other was dark, with skin as pale and white as the full
moon in winter.

'While Golden Hair excelled in all strength, hunting, leaping,
wrestling and the powers of arms and health, Dark Hair could
charm the birds out of the bushes with his voice and verse, and
knew the secret life of roots and under-stones as intimately as he
knew of the black hairs upon his pale arms.

'Golden Hair delighted in the chase, the hunt, until the
shapely, curved red deer fled at the sound of his joyous horn; but
Dark Hair sat and spoke with the timid animals through the quiet

shadowed night. Because of his strange, gentle ways, Dark Hair was feared by other, lesser, men.

'But not by women. For women flowed towards both brothers, light and dark, as water down an easy slope. Never a day or night was passing without sensuous delights, laughing, hot thighs, gasps in feather-filled beds. You might imagine, if you know anything at all about life (which you surely do not) that they are going to fall out over a woman. Not so.

'When they did argue, for dispute was bound to arise between those two who loved one another until even wind and water were jealous of their love, it was not over a woman. After all, why should those brothers dispute over a mere woman, when all women in that broad fair land were their own for the asking and the taking and the having?

'No. Although it is said by foolish ignorant people, far lost to the truth, that these two brothers fought over a woman, and even that she herself encouraged their fighting to the death, it was no woman, I say, that led to the strife and the misery that I shall now relate.

'It was upon a wild and surprising day that Dark Hair rode into the hall where his mother sat chewing hemp. Right in on horseback he rode, as was the curious habit of those simple, noble, old dirty days. As the doting servants led his steed away to one of the gilded stalls that surrounded the interior of the hall, for humans and animals slept together in those rough times, Dark Hair slowly walked up to his mother's chair. His head was bowed and his hand was upon his sword hilt; he shed doom and sorrow about him as freely as a hedgehog sheds fleas. His observant mother spat out her wad of hemp, and paused in her complex weaving, looking hard at her son and at his doom.

'As she laid her loom to rest, daylight wavered for the passing of one heartbeat, and the horses around the hall stamped and whinnied with delight, which was a soul-shrivelling sound to hear.

'"Well, dark-haired boy," said the mother, "what news do you bring to your waiting mother? I can see that it is not good, but perhaps it will not be too bad either. Where have you been all this long wild day?"

'"Oh mother . . . I have been out hunting."

'"Hunting, you? This is strange indeed, I knowing that you have never hunted nor killed an animal in your short life. Show me your sword!" And upon her inescapable command, he drew that bright blade only one finger span out of the royal blue and green enamelled scabbard, to show her that it was rich with dark clotted blood. At the smell of this blood, the horses craned their long lovely necks, and edged closer, champing hard and grinding their white teeth, curling up their long dark lips.

'"And what, lovely boy, did you kill with that hard sword?"

'"Oh mother, it was a little bird that lacked any singing."

'"Indeed and was it so? Indeed and it was not . . . a little bird's blood could never be as red as that blood that draws the horses so from out of their gilded stalls. Tell again, and improve in the telling of your hunting."

'"Oh mother, it was a little grey mare that lacked for running."

'"Indeed and was it so? Indeed and it was not . . . a little grey mare's blood could never be so rich as this blood that draws the horses out of their gilded stalls and then closer and closer yet. Nor would they champ and spoil to lick the blood of one of their own kind. Tell again, dark haired gentle boy, and improve in the telling of your hunting!"

'"Oh mother, it is the blood of my own dearest brother who rode away with me this day!"

'At this the horses reared up and screamed, and struck the flint flagstones with their hard crystal-shod hooves until showers of sparks flew in all directions. Very still then this woman sat before her great loom, until at last she asked, in a most quiet voice, "What did you two fall out about, son, come tell it unto me?"

'"Oh it was that he plucked up a little hazel bush that should have grown to a tree." At this a great silence fell upon the horses, and they bowed their strong sleek necks and wept pure tears until sweet clean water ran over the flint flagstones to all four corners of the world.

'"And what will you do as penance, my son? My son, come tell it unto me?"

'"Oh, I'll set my foot in a bottomless boat and sail across the sea."

'"And when will you be coming back again, son, come tell it unto me?"

'"When the Moon and the Sun dance together on the hill, and that you will never see!" And with these words Dark Hair flung off out of that place, and was never seen again.'

Windfall listened to this nonsense with utter scorn.

'E moxi sexop miopd nafm u najjy nyipt os hu joca!' he said angrily.

The elder paused before replying, as if he masterfully re-strained himself from picking Windfall up by the throat and flinging him headlong down into the great steaming vent by which they sat.

'Then your life has not yet been lived, that's all I can say in reply to your accusation. It was exactly and precisely all this plucking up and swording down, clearly defined in the story which I have just told you, that caused the very rattling and dumbness of the world wherein you and yours think that they are living . . . take my word for it.'

'Goy wmiy daun y ijj hos? Wm an I ypoo na hrapysy?'

'Because not long after the world had finished shaking, only a few very small trees had their roots in reality, that's why. Those few trees were the only way to find any truth, something which people don't bother with today, but which the simple folk of those times seemed to think was important. To pluck up such a tree, and I would have you notice that it was plucked up, not cut down, was to literally deprive the world of life, and not only the world of that time and place, but quite a large number of other worlds too.'

'Pjoyt n puayd os ognapxyus, osd sy ypoan peoyd is pjoyt.'

'Hmm, well you may revel in such idiotic and pompous thoughts until the last cow comes home, but you are lost among the lost if you live by them. But I've only told you the known half of the story.'

'In ymup hpi, a pexepod sfanyap?'

'There is the untold part, you snail-brained spittlewit. Any story has two natural parts, the told part and the untold part. Now if you did not immediately pick up the untold part, I being the champion story-teller of my generation, then the wit to pick it up is probably far beyond you, or totally lacking within you. You missed, let me remind you, the important parts when you were upstairs, eh? Now be sensible for a change and ask me the obvious question . . .?'

'Wmy un ym usyad ripy ci m nyept?'

'A good question, my lad, a good question. When the golden haired brother pulled up the little tree, he did indeed deprive his people of their sole access to unmanifest reality, to the under-neath that makes all worlds wherever and whenever they are or are not. If you follow me. Therefore it was his dark brother's sad duty to dispatch him immediately to bring back a tree from underneath, where they naturally come up from, to replace that shrub which he plucked up. So far so good?

'However, as was frequently the way of things after the earth shook and the sky fell and much of the land was swallowed by sea, the one who was sent was the one who should have stayed. And the one who stayed was the one who should have been sent, except, of course, that Dark Hair would never have done anything so foolish in the first place to occasion any such sending. Out of this ultimate inelegant confusion of cause and effect, arising from a flippant folly, came a large number of apparent problems which have hardly been resolved to this very day.'

'Uy ijj naesdn joke susnasno y ha, oc tu wojj evfen ho nnopyees!' said Windfall firmly.

'Assert away, assert away. At least you are voicing some kind of opinion at last, no matter how bucolic and inept it may be. Yes, no matter how feeble your assertion, it is superior to being silent. The point of the story was, and is, and always will be, and goodness knows how you managed to miss it, it being as vividly noticeable as a peeled severed head stuck upon a spike at a crossroads, that the bright one became hopelessly lost underneath. So lost, where he had been sent, (much as you think you are lost now, though of course you are not even one fraction as lost as you think or one shaving of a fraction as lost as you might be and probably will be) that his dark brother had to be sent in after him!'

'Nosy os acyup mh? Kojjd?'

'That is exactly what I mean, my lad, exactly. You see the dark one was so *suitable* that he stood a far better chance of recovering that which had been lost than his bright brother did.'

Windfall remembered this word *suitable* from other occasions, and was suddenly prompted to ask, 'Asd ym wuhes, wmy rapy dad nmu rojt?'

But with these rash, brash, foolish words, there arose a great gout of steam from the deep vent by which they had been conversing so pleasantly, relaxing and telling tales. It began to bubble and spout at an alarming rate, with water welling up after the steam and flooding over the containing wall. The old man picked up a stout stick that lay by his feet, and began beating at the rising water with great vigour, as if expecting it to retreat below to avoid his assault. But it rose without pausing for breath, until both teller and listener were up to their knees, then up to their waists, then up to their necks.

'Bloody thing always does this if some idiot asks the wrong

question', grunted the elder, treading water expertly. 'Why couldn't you have just slipped it to the old owl and her snaky daughter up there? I don't know, at one time men had some blood and thrust, now they just flop and whimper. So just relax, and let the water float you up to the roof. If you push hard on the central panel up there, it might, perhaps, open up for you. It's the same hatchway that mother and daughter would have tipped you down anyway when they'd finished with you. So you'll be more or less back where you began . . . if you're a lucky man they'll still be there, finishing off the mead and panting for it. So get on and be *suitable*.

'If, on the other hand, you are an unlucky man, and I make no comment at this point, then they will be out, and you'll just have to find some other way around your terrible inability.' With these enigmatic words the rising water reached the uppermost level of the lamps, and with a loud hissing stink of snuffed wicks, the chamber was plunged into total steaming darkness.

'Wmp ro tae dusy jeax hi!' cried Windfall, tears springing to his already wet eyes and merging unnoticed with the hot flooding water. 'Fhu gofk! Mujr hu!'

He had lost the first man who had spoken to him compassionately, as if he was another intelligent adult, the first man he had ever truly loved.

'Don't worry about me,' came the old man's voice faintly, wetly, 'I've done this before. Just remember to push when you get up there . . .'

THE DREAM OF SAINT AUSTIN

Satire plays a small but important part in poetry, story-telling, and esoteric arts. Ancient poets and satirists in Ireland, for example, were feared for their powers, and a satirized man or woman could not live within society; great princes and chieftains went in dread of being satirized by Druids, who could lay them low forever with a well-placed verse, phrase, or epithet. Modern satire seems, with some noteable exceptions, to be less damaging to public figures than was the ancient sort.

As in 'How a Book was Found', this tale, 'The Dream of Saint Austin', refers to the apocryphal Gospel of Mary Magdalene, using the mysterious book as an emblem for whatever was removed from orthodox Christianity through its increasing politicization. Saint Austin, who is not of course any historical saint such as Augustine of Canterbury or Augustine of Hippo, is a dreamlike saint in a mocking dream, who encounters a mysterious woman. She leads him upon a bizarre journey into the future, with many surprises, exchanges of left and right, and enough dream-symbols to fill a psychotherapist with deep joy.

Of course, the saint, for whom our story-teller cannot find sufficient superlatives, totally misunderstands his dream within a dream, and despite the warnings of the mysterious woman, he decides, upon awakening, to expunge the heretical text which he has been examining from all orthodox use. The rest, of course, is history.

One last note, for the really devious among you; this is the same story as 'Ride the Wind's Back' on page 137, with the same location, the same main characters, and the same implications. But they are completely different from one another.

THE DREAM OF SAINT AUSTIN

It happened one evening that the blessed holy Saint Austin sat reading from a book, and the book that he read from was the

Gospel of Mary Magdalene. Following each line carefully with his finger, and whispering each word to himself, he had just reached that part of the gospel where Mary carries off the sacred girl child, to keep her hidden from the soldiers of Rome. What with the large supper that he had eaten and the warmth of the great reninous logs burning in the wide hearth, the good, saintly and virtuous man began to drift into a gentle well-deserved sleep.

In that comfortable sleep, Saint Austin dreamed that he was awake. He stood just outside his own humble doorway in the light of early morning, ready to turn a corner into whatever new experience the day might offer. The kind and patient holy man stepped out briskly to walk about and survey the town. On the corner, where a great carved archway filled with the faces of despicable pagan false gods leapt over the roadway, he met with a small woman.

This small woman stood as if waiting for the wise and prudent saint; she was wrapped about in a faded green coat and hood, with the hood pulled up until it all but hid her face. As Saint Austin drew near, stepping briskly and breathing deeply, she spoke directly to him.

'And where do you think you are?' she asked boldly, without any introduction or seeking of benediction, 'And where might you think that you are going on this fine morning?'

'I know exactly where I am', the saint replied, astonished and mildly offended at such boldness and directness from a woman, 'and I intend to make my own way as God wills . . .' But she caught him, taking his right elbow in a tight pinch between her left finger and thumb. She spoke in a firm voice.

'You might think that you are *here*, or that you are going in some specific direction, and that *there*, wherever it is, is where you want to go . . . but you are mistaken.' Saint Austin looked at her sharp hooked nose sticking out from the shadows of her faded green hood; wriggle as he might he could not free himself from her terrible grip.

'I do not understand', said the pure and thrifty saint. 'What are you saying?' His elbow ached with the sensation of dull glowing fire. The small woman shook her head sadly.

'Hhhrrngmmnpch' she said, a long gargling breathing and snorting-liquid sound from deep in her throat, and all in Welsh, though previously they had spoken only Latin. 'Well, if you really cannot see what is in front of your face, I shall have to show it to you in a dream.'

And so in his dream in which he dreamed of himself to be awake, the pure Saint Austin fell asleep and dreamed another dream, just as the small green-covered woman had said. In this dream he was also wide-awake, and being pushed along hard by a strange short woman in a faded green coat and hood. She walked just behind him, gripping his right elbow hard between her left finger and thumb, pushing all the time and steering him wherever she wanted him to go. He could not quite see her, but she kept up a commentary upon their progress with every stage of the walk.

'You see?' she croaked, 'You see where you have come to now?' Saint Austin looked about him, and found himself to be in a large square, built up with immense houses, no, palaces, of stone, each having many fine glass-filled windows. In the centre of the square was a neatly trimmed area of green grass, upon which many dogs disported themselves shamelessly. In the centre of this green a tall obelisk reared upwards, pointing its needle of stone towards a murky sky tinged with yellow and grey. A finer monument, purloined from some vassal kingdom long ago, might not have been seen in Rome itself.

Out of the very corner of his limpid clear eye, Saint Austin could glimpse rushing brightly-coloured shapes, hurtling around the wide level road of that fine square at great speed. They moved with such unseemly rapidity that it was certain they would crash into one another, yet they remained apart. The small woman, who possessed considerable vigour when it came to talking while pinching, pushed and hopped Saint Austin through this startling cavalcade unscathed. If he had been alone, his well-shaped mouth might have hung open in amazement, but in female company he preserved and manifested his innate dignity, and kept his lips tight shut, even compressed slightly.

The woman pushed and then pulled him back to a sudden halt, directly in front of one of the tall palaces. It stood with its handsome wooden and glass doors flung wide open.

'*Now* do you see?' she demanded, giving his right elbow a neat little twitch and sending shooting pains up his well-proportioned arm and through his noble skull into his left ear, '*That* is where you are truly going!'

Upon the door of the palace was a fine inscription in a language that the intelligent and learned saint did not know, yet even as he gazed sternly upon the letters, they resolved themselves into these words: The Institute of Transpersonal Development, Inc. This seemed an odd, essentially meaningless label to the holy man, for it implied that the spirit could somehow grow without or beyond the soul.

Somewhere beyond two dreams, or before a dream within a dream, Saint Austin turned a page in his warm firelit room, and still drowsing, read slowly of how Mary Magdalene had hidden the sacred girl child in a cave to await the arrival of her brother.

'Pay attention to what I say', a dry penetrating voice cut into his reverie, 'and look at the mess you will get them all into if you do not truly know where you are going . . .'

Saint Austin walked in through the open door of that great school, embedded within his dreaming dream of wakefulness, and found that many classes were in progress. Large numbers of youths and maidens, yes, even young women, attired in meagre garishly-coloured immodest costumes transacted money to learn from teachers. Here was a remarkable example of competent organization for eminently laudable ends; yet he could not grasp why money changed hands for that which was, or should be, free as air or water.

Even as he drew this perspicacious analogy, he felt his right elbow jerk and twitch with pain, and a voice wheezed into his right ear, 'Hachmychngdd!' or so it sounded to him. 'In this place they pay for everything, even water itself. And if they want any clean air they must be very wealthy indeed to afford a house in a place that has any . . .'

The good saint walked on through that wonderful building, where numerous friendly, bright young persons filled his hands with books, papers, and dozens of remarkably but poorly tinted pictures. As each item was added to the pile, as each voice gabbled forth its message of good news, realization, integration and individuation, he began to feel an increasing pain in his left foot. Looking down, the saint found that he had become entrapped in a strange wooden snare, constructed from a complex pattern of interlinked sticks. These sticks seemed, at first glance, to be loosely assembled, but try as he might, the nimble and graceful Saint Austin could not shake off this curious object. As his arms were now heavily laden with books, folders, images, packages, lists, schedules, and summaries, he could not stoop to take it off. Shake off or take off, he muttered to himself.

Suddenly Saint Austin found that he was walking along a back corridor in the building, dragging his wooden snare along in a shuffling kind of hopping motion, clutching his bundle of books and papers in both arms, with his right elbow pulled slightly out of joint and aching as if someone just out of sight held it in a tight pinching grip.

He entered a brightly lit vault, in which many people in white blood-stained aprons scurried about purposefully. They pushed and wrestled long pinkish-grey slabs of meat into clear membraneous sacks, and stuffed the packages into little metal cupboards or chests that lined the walls. The air seemed cold, and the saint's sweet breath steamed, yet he had been certain that it was summer outside on the grand square, with its green grass sporting dogs and central obelisk.

'*Now* do you see what will happen?' asked a voice, close to his right ear. He looked hard, and realized that the anonymous objects being moved were bodies, deprived of their clothes and hair, and that they were being fed into long boxes full of ice. The fine school at the front of this building seemed to subsist on these poor plucked creatures frozen away in the vaults beneath. A most horrible revelation.

'At last' said the irritating voice of a woman, 'at last you can see where you are going . . . or where you will go if you are not very very careful.'

Determined to escape, Saint Austin manfully flung down the stack of books which he unwillingly carried and kicked the snare from his foot; he ran out of the fine building, knocking smiling youths and maidens to the finely polished, brightly-coloured floor. Leaping out of the wide front door of that terrible place, he found himself back upon the corner of his own street, close to the soaring archway with its offensive images of false gods, still evident even after vigilant attacks by true believers armed with hammers, stones, ladders, and styli. A small woman wrapped in a green coat and deep hood stood directly in front of his own doorway. A woman!

'Now be a good boy,' she croaked, 'Be a good boy for a change, and try to remember what I've shown you.'

Saint Austin awoke with a sudden jolt, feeling as if he had fallen hard into his chair. His foot and both his elbows ached, and his right ear tingled abominably. The Gospel that he had been reading almost dropped out of his thin eloquent and demonstrative hands. The pages fell open to that place where the divinely royal brother and sister, still tiny children, set sail to the West along with their great uncle. A harsh dry voice still seemed to buzz faintly in his head, fading away even as he fully woke.

Had he been dreaming?

Now in full command of his awesome faculties, the saint set the beautifully hand-scribed and illuminated volume upon a stout stand, well away, for the moment, from the heat of the fire. Time to sleep, he reflected. Time to rest, and tomorrow he would begin to dictate a strict programme for the expurgation of this heretical dangerous doctrine, so clearly stated within the damnable book that he had been reading. It would be declared to be nonsense, and removed entirely from circulation.

THE FAIRY HARP

Some powerful traditional motifs are woven into this tale, concerning the realm of Fairy, the inhabitants and topography of that realm, the acquisition of magical objects (in this case a Fairy Harp), and the perplexing aid of phantom allies.

The means of descent into the Otherworld, drawn from Gaelic tradition and made by our unwitting hero in a dream, is still used in visualizations today, and is a classic example of how a traditional image can be employed in both story-telling and active meditation and visualization.

The mysterious cryptic language of Fives makes another appearance here, including a longer passage appended to the end of the tale, for those who wish to pursue its meaning further.

Like most dealings with the land or people of Fairy, this magical tale is the merest summary of an event that led to a complex set of adventures. The central character is not, of course, myself.

THE FAIRY HARP

Do you have a flair, a talent for finding things? I do . . . or rather, I used to. For years I would wake up and know which junkshop, market, sale, to attend. I suppose that I still have that flair now, but have not used it for some time, being occupied with other matters. My house is crammed with prints, carvings, and thousands of books . . . mostly found through following a blind intuition. Of course, most of it is rubbish, and only of interest to me, though some of the books and prints have values that increase with absurd speed.

Yes, it is an interesting talent; but there is an old adage, hoary wisdom, that we always pay a price for such gifts. This becomes

even more bitter when the mild gift gives a greater gift; then the price is heavy indeed. But I run ahead of myself here, a bad habit which I am unable to avoid. So I shall return to the time and place wherein my gift found me a gift, and though the first price, the monetary one, seemed small, the true price was, and is, high.

On a hot sweating day, a Saturday in midsummer, I knew that I had to go to the local antique market . . . which is a euphemism for junk and bric-a-brac sale. Something, my talent told me, waited there for me. An eighteenth-century history book, perhaps, useless to anyone but an obscure author such as myself, a curious walking stick, or, more rare in these avaricious collectorified times, an old musical instrument. I have a music room replete with bagpipes, mandolines, Syrian *ouds*, hammered dulcimers, shawms, old flutes, concertinas, fretless banjos and frail Victorian guitars that never seem to have been played, still redolent of delicate ladies and their musical fashions. All bought for modest sums, and now valuable to collectors or dealers . . . but as I am a musician, and was a musician for years before becoming an author, I have no intention of speculating unless, as sometimes becomes necessary, it be to raise money to buy another instrument.

So I strolled around the market, waiting for my hands to twitch. Oh yes, when I come close to the object which my talent has located from afar, my hands twitch slightly. Parapsychic greed, perhaps.

One stall in particular seemed promising, as it had several large cardboard boxes of books unsorted and unpriced by the dealer . . . all the best bargains come this way. Once I found a printed translation of the medieval *History of Glastonbury* by William of Malmesbury. Not very interesting in itself, as there are several editions of this famous book which describes, among other wonders, the (falsified) finding of King Arthur's tomb by the monks of the Abbey. But this happened to be the personal copy belonging, once, to Frederick Bligh Bond, the archaeologist who excavated Glastonbury Abbey in the early twentieth century, according to some very unorthodox theories.

Though proven correct in his archaeological work, and vindicated by the actual finds that he had predicted accurately, Bligh Bond was so publicly ridiculed for his esoteric leanings that he eventually left Britain for America. But somehow his little book remained behind, finding its way by devious routes into my hands. He had made copious pencil notes in every margin, giving insights into many aspects of his own work, and into the lives of other mystics of the period, including Fiona Macleod (the poetic pseydonym of William Sharp), and J. Giles, who translated many of the ancient chronicles from Latin into English in the late nineteenth century. This annotated book also described certain meetings, and the founding of a spiritual order . . . but that is another story.

So I dug into the boxes of books, hoping to find something of comparable interest at a price low enough to encourage purchase. The dealer was a rather loutish character, smelling of beer even at ten in the morning, unshaven, and sniffing liquidly. I liked him immediately. But after twenty or thirty books on subjects such as water board reports for 1933 in the county of Hampshire, weighty verse dramas by self-published poets, fully indexed guides to the transactions of the Metallurgical Society of Great Britain and Ireland (1897–1912), and many dull moralistic novels, I paused.

Looking up, I saw the dealer hurriedly slip his can under the table, as if he was afraid that I might like a beer for myself. This was a delicate moment, for he knew that I was about to ask for something specific, and (assuming it was not beer) that if he could establish my desires he could certainly fix a higher price than that possible from a casual purchaser.

'Ah . . hmm . . . do you ever have any old musical instruments?' I murmured indifferently while flipping through a copy of *Women's Own* from 1967 as if it really interested me and musical instruments were merely an aside or a flippant question to pass away some time between other more important matters. It may have been my imagination, or so I thought at the time, but he seemed to flinch as if he had been slapped in the face. He looked at me for a long time before replying.

'Musician, are you?' he finally grunted.

'Yes,' I admitted, knowing that this would be better for pricing anything than being a collector or, heaven forbid, a dealer.

'Well, I've got a crate of old stuff in the van. The usual, you know, bought it as a lot in the auction last week. Sheet music, a few books on music, some letters; there's an old mandolin and a beaten up kind of harp, more of a toy really. You could have the lot for say . . . a hundred quid.' He looked at me sideways, as if to estimate the effect of this opening figure.

'I'd like to take a look,' I said casually, my fingers twitching so hard that I crammed my hands into my pockets. Whatever I had come for was in that crate . . . but if he was asking a hundred pounds, then it meant that he had probably paid fifteen or twenty for the lot, and would not settle for less than sixty. He was back within a few minutes, staggering under a large wooden crate, which he slammed, quite deliberately, down onto the concrete floor. Something gave a loud discordant twang from inside.

'Go on then, take look. But I'm not splitting it up, it's all or nothing . . . hundred quid, round figure. Cost me ninety, so I'm not really making anything, just enough for my petrol to get here today. Take a good look . . .' And his hand slid cunningly towards the beer can even as I delved into the crate.

Of course, I found it straight away. The surrounding sheet music, by worthies such as Ethelbert Nevin, seemed to slide away. The broken mandolin fell into one corner, and revealed a small dull brown harp, with a bundle of letters tied with green silk ribbon to the forepillar. It was plain, almost ugly, made with only fifteen strings. But as I touched it, it seemed to tremble, to shift slightly into my hands. This was what I had come for.

But there was a problem . . . the price. Now if it had merely been a chance-found instrument or set of books, I could have haggled with the dealer, but when something is found by flair, by talent, you have to pay the actual price asked or leave it be. A hundred was too much, and I had to somehow find out the real price without conflict, otherwise I was in breach of talent and might lose my minor psychic skill forever. Remember, no gift without a price.

'I like the harp,' I said, clutching it tightly and emerging from the crate. This time he openly took a long pull on his beer, and sat back with a look of clear satisfaction on his face.

'Of course,' I continued hurriedly, 'it's only a home-made thing, perhaps an amateur kit or hobby instrument . . . it would need a lot of work. What about selling me the harp on its own?'

'Sorry matey, can't be done. You buy the sheet music and the mandolin, and I'll *give* you the harp, but I want to be shot of the lot. Hundred quid. Tell you what, ninety-five for cash no receipt.'

I waited, desperate to take the harp home, desperate to open that package of letters and see what they contained. But I waited.

'Tell you what . . . I saw you looking through the books there, take a look at these, perhaps we can make a deal on the lot.' And with this he pulled a cardboard box out from beneath the table, right next to his now depleted six-pack of beer. And like a conjuror, he placed two large blue books upon the table-top. My fingers twitched again, but only slightly. They were copies of William Phelps' *History of Somerset* published in the nineteenth century.

'I'll throw these in as well, can't get rid of them . . . there are some nice prints in them though. You could make a bob or two framing them to sell . . . ninety quid for the lot, and the harp is free.' He stressed the gift of the harp, as if it was important, and then, in a rush of frank confession, said, 'To tell you the truth, that's how I got it. Somebody's deceased estate . . . they was to give the harp away to whoever would take it . . . but the executors put it in to sell with a load of other stuff . . . conditional, like.'

I watched my hands count out nine new ten pound notes. I sold the mandolin and the sheet music to a dealer further down the market for fifteen pounds cash, no receipt. And with the small harp under one arm, The *History of Somerset* under the other, and the bundle of faded letters in my now hollow cash-depleted pocket, I walked out into the stifling heat of the city in midsummer.

On arriving home, I gave the books only the briefest of attention; they were a complete history of Somerset in considerable detail, from prehistoric times to the nineteenth century, and contained much of interest to the historian, antiquarian, or archaeologist. They were certainly a bargain at whatever proportion of the ninety pounds they had cost. I suddenly realized that these books alone might be worth fifty or sixty or more to a collector, and I had already made fifteen back by selling the bundle of sheet music (also collectable) and the broken mandolin. And the harp . . . well, he had stressed that the harp came free, and insisted on shaking hands upon it all. As I left he had been opening his last beer and smiling.

So, at last, I sat in the quiet of my music room, and untied the green silk ribbon that held the bundle of letters against the forepillar of the harp. I set them carefully down and turned to look first at the instrument. All fifteen strings were intact and curiously made of brass, copper, or some similar wire, blackened with age but still gleaming in places. I rubbed at this patina, and the strings reappeared as bright golden wires of varying gauges, the bass strings being braided and wound to gain thickness and timbre.

The fifteen tuning pins in the harmonic curve were also black, but with a little hard rubbing with a cloth appeared, to my considerable surprise, to be silver. This dull brown instrument had hidden material qualities. The wood appeared to be oak for the forepillar, and sycamore for the curve. The sound box was carved out of one piece, in the very ancient manner of true Celtic harps, and was of a dark black wood of uncertain type. The sound board was dark brown, with a few stains as if of rusty water, and seemed to be pine or spruce. All good quality materials, plain, undecorated, old.

Finally I ran my hand along the fifteen strings. They produced a mellow but discordant sound, and I reached for my tuning keys. None of them fitted the small silver pins. So I turned to the faded envelopes, and in the first, wrapped in a thick soft fabric like woven grass, there was a bronze tuning key, very ornately wrought with convoluted twists and spirals and shapes. It fitted the silver tuning pins perfectly, and I spent some time setting the strings into a two-octave scale. If you know stringed instruments well, you can physically *feel* the pitch and manner in which they are accustomed to be tuned and the wood settles happily to its familiar tension and shape. The pitch required was low, the scale somehow indeterminate, with no thought of modern tempering.

The sound of that harp was like a lovely voice from another world, from a distant dream-past. I wondered who could have owned such a sweet instrument, and so opened the letters at last, hoping to find some history of the instrument therein . . .

That night I had a vivid and disturbing dream, so real and terrifying that I awoke with a jolt, feeling that I had slammed back into my bed after falling from a height. In the dream I was crawling among the roots of a great tree, thick, knotted, rough, boled roots like branches, yet roots they were, stretching and weaving around me into a wide web of tangles and grasping stems. Yet I was not within the earth, for the roots seemed to grow upwards to the sky above, and a strong gravity pulled me ever towards their centre, their origin, which was below me wherever I turned.

As I struggled, crawling aimlessly, twisting and turning one way then another, seeking a way out of the mazy root grip, rasping my hands, tearing my clothes, I suddenly looked down. Far below me I saw the trunk of a mighty tree seeming to fall away, and then spread out into a wide cone, a mountain, a circle of shivering green and silver branches and leaves. The height was terrifying, and my sweating hands slipped upon the rootbark.

I awoke, sweating indeed in my midsummer night bed in the centre of the unsleeping city. Nor could I sleep again until dawn and the cool wind that rises at that time. Whenever I closed my eyes I felt myself falling, falling down a huge smooth brown-barked tree trunk, down towards the hard ground far below.

The following evening, the weather being still hot and fine, I brought out my polishing kit for the restoration of varnishes and finishes on wooden instruments. The black body, brown fore-pillar and stained sound board of the little harp deserved a thorough cleaning. The rusty stains upon the fine grained sound board could, perhaps, be removed, with a mixture of two parts malt vinegar, two of linseed oil, and three parts methylated spirits. Or so I thought.

The sound box and forepillar cleaned well and began to glow under my attentions, but the sound board, though much dirt came from it, retained its complex red watermarks. I began to wonder if they were within the wood rather than upon it. In certain lights the stain looked like two faces, in others like a map of two adjoining zones, linked by a thin line.

I tuned the harp several times and found that it stayed well in tune once it had settled. The wire strings were gleaming now and seemed to be an alloy of brass, though they shone like gold. I knew that some very early instruments had indeed been strung with gold wires, but considered this highly unlikely for such a plain and functional harp, surely dating from no earlier than the last century.

With this thought in mind I turned again to the letters.

'*I would have you take especial care of the harp,*' the first one had read the previous day, '*for it is of great value to its owner, and he or she will never be without a co-walker. Yours in both . . .*' and then one of those stylized complex signatures that was illegible to all except those who knew the writer. No address or date, but the writing was bold and heavily looped, one of the formal hands used at a guess in the eighteenth or nineteenth century. So the instrument was that old. The letter was not addressed to anyone either, no 'Dear so and so', no 'Beloved . . .' I recognized the phrase *co-walker* from somewhere, but could not place it, and *yours in both . . .* was obviously an abbreviation of some phrase known to the reader, but its expansion escaped me. There were three further letters, in the same hand. All were surprising, strange, tantalizingly cryptic.

The Second Letter

A harper wandered by the sea shore, and there he found the body of a beautiful girl, drowned and rotted in the salt waters. He cut off her golden hair and braided it up into harp strings: he took her fine finger bones to make harp seating pins; and her body he floated out into the mother deep to rest.

When he came to a great hall that night, he fitted his dark wooden harp with the golden hair strings and the fine white bone pins to seat them into the sounding board. The harp struck up of its own accord, and sang:

> *Woe unto my sister*
> *Woe unto my sister*
> *Woe unto my sister*

And a lovely dark-haired brown-eyed girl in the court screamed aloud and ran headlong from the hall. But the lord and lady of that place set the great ban-dogs after her, for she had murdered her own sister out of spite and jealousy and all for love of a mortal man. The dogs tore her to pieces. The next morning the harper flung his harp into the great river, and it was washed away, floating upon the waters for many days and nights.

And in a hollow of a deep pool made by an old mill dam, long overgrown with willows, the harp came to rest. And there it was found.

I took this curious opening to be the beginning of a story or perhaps a florid novel by the original owner of the little harp, a fantasy based upon his or her instrument. It reminded me of an old ballad, of a children's dance-game. Though sceptically telling myself that I was a fool, I could not resist looking at the mounting pins on the harp, those used to seat the strings firmly in their holes through the sound board. They were of, I think, ivory. But the strings were certainly wire and not hair.

That night I was in the tree again. No sooner had I fallen asleep than I found myself trapped and crawling, fumbling through the roots. The only way accessible seemed to be downwards, where they grew thicker and wider, merging into the trunk. I was always forced to travel that way, with my head downwards, though I wanted to turn and climb up, up to ordinary sky above . . . the sky that meant my home, the sky over my house in the waking world.

My knees were stuck under my chin, my arms pinned by two

great dark roots. I heaved my body through the narrow space
between them, and found that I had again moved down towards
the trunk. I twisted my head around and saw that I was not alone.
Sitting upon a wide major root to my left was a dead girl: her eyes
had long been nibbled away by fishes, her flesh was puffed and
white, her head bald of hair. Yet she turned towards me, and
pointing one fingerless hand downwards, and the other upwards, opened her mouth, revealing green teeth.

'*Ymo gany wit er un daws*,' she said in a sweet clear voice. I knew
exactly what this meant, though it was no language I had ever
heard before: I would only be free if I climbed down the trunk
of the great tree.

Then, to my great relief, I awoke.

The Third Letter

*No harpist should be without a consoling song or verse. I commend
this rhyme to you, wherever you may find yourself. Yours in both . . .*

> *In fives I run against the sun*
> *My spirit lost, two children gone.*
> *My tongue direct is now enchained*
> *Five crossed the bridge*
> *Yet still remained.*

This short message, quite incomprehensible, was accompanied
by a detailed illustration, finely drawn in ink. It showed a fertile
landscape with a river flowing through it. Lying by the river bank
was a large naked woman of the proportions preferred by
Reubens. She seemed to be asleep. A horde of children scam-
pered to and fro over a bridge, while a wild capering man with
bald head, seamed wrinkled face and ragged beard led them over
the river. He clutched a collection of fine chains attached, as it
seemed, to their tongues. He danced backwards over the bridge
towards the far bank, drawing some of the children with him,
while others ran in the opposite direction. Five rather forlorn-
looking infants stood by the sleeping woman, fingering their
chainless tongues.

After reading the curious missive and studying the picture, I
refrained for some time from opening the fourth and last letter,
hardly daring to guess what nonsense it might contain. And it
was only then, when I finally opened that fourth envelope of rich
creamy paper, that I realized that they had all been sealed: they

were not the keepsakes, the love letters that I had assumed them to be, but were unopened communications . . . no one had read them before they had come into my possession.

I tried once again to clean the stains from the sound board of the harp, but the more I cleaned the more dirt came from the native wood, leaving the red marks intact. I tried looking at them in a mirror, holding the instrument up to catch the light; they reminded me more than ever of a map, of the sort drawn before the introduction of modern contours, with shaded hills and valleys, tracts of forest, mysterious blank areas. I had seen as much, I reminded myself, upon my bedroom ceiling as a child.

That night I began to climb down the tree trunk, shaking with fear, almost paralysed with vertigo. It plummeted away below me, finally opening out into a vast cone of branches and glittering leaves, trembling in the distant wind below. As I emerged from the roots, clambering around onto the base of the trunk, I found that there were deep folds in the bark, and that these made precarious toeholds. As is the way with dreams, I began to climb down the trunk face-first, as if I had no common sense to turn round and climb normally.

I emerged from out of the shade of the roots into bright light, of a clarity and quality that I had never experienced before. I could see every detail in the tree bark, every tiny swirl and hue of colour from dark black through brown to subtle reds and pinks, with occasional flushes of rich green. I could see every fold and pattern of the skin of my hands, and the fine hairs normally invisible upon them. So clear was my vision in that light that I began to laugh for sheer pleasure, realizing how grey and clouded it had been before. As I laughed I climbed boldly down, and the wind hit me.

I had seen the leaves shimmering far below but had not realized the strength of wind necessary to shake them: it laid hold of me and began to push me around the tree trunk to my left, whipping my clothes, tearing at my hair. My eyes filled with tears, and even my mouth was pulled sideways, and my nails began to break and bleed where I gripped hard upon the tree trunk.

Suddenly I was determined that, come what may — vertigo, gales, sea-dead maidens uttering gibberish — I would climb down that tree into the branches below and onto the ground beyond that. Even as I made this resolution, I could see that a wide land spread out far below, and the wind whipped my head around until I saw a low rounded hill far across the grassy plain. I awoke to a strange humming wailing sound that rose and fell without rhythm. I staggered from my bed and felt the night wind blowing through the open window, bringing with it the first rain for weeks. It blew against the strings of the little harp where I had set it by my bedside, and this eerie resonance had surely influenced my dream. In future, I said to myself, picking up the harp, this stays in the music room where it belongs.

And yet somehow I knew that it did not belong in the music room, irrational though the notion was. It belonged . . . I took the harp into the kitchen with me, and made coffee. Where did it belong, if not in a music room?

The Fourth Letter

The fourth letter had been useless to me, to say the least. It began as follows:

'*Oc tiu mixa gaas igja ya ypisjiye yma fada ac Cixon taa wijj buas cpab paudisb ymin jiyyip . . .*' — and proceeded accordingly for a further short page of neat stylish handwriting. If you wish to read the rest, and struggle with its meaning as I did, I have appended it to the end of this preliminary account of my adventures. Suffice it to say I could not read the message for some time, and by the time I could read it I knew most of what was in it from hard experience. It ended, as with the previous letters, with the words '*Yours in both worlds*' and the florid illegible signature, which I later discovered to simply be the words '*A Friend*'.

But I was into my third almost sleepless night, and by the fourth day I was exhausted. My work was suffering, and I found myself falling asleep, or rather jolting awake, when I should have been proof-reading. The rain was short lived, and the heat wave reasserted itself. I ran deep cold baths, did press-ups, even jogged around the block, much to the amusement of my neighbours who knew that I was an effete arty type. I waited for night.

Late in the evening, the sun shines horizontally into the western windows of my house, tunnelled and reflected from the tall pale sandstone walls of the surrounding buildings, giving a red-tinged level light that is unusual, distinctive. It was in that light that I slept, and found myself half-way down the great tree.

In my previous dreams, in the middle of the night, it had been bright noon in the tree place, but now it was early dawn. A pure blue-green light swept up over the land below, so fast that the shadows seemed to run before it. Looking down I saw dim shapes running to keep within the receding shadows, but when I looked again they had vanished, and I thought that I had been mistaken.

As the dawnlight increased, I wandered among the branches, and found them at last to widen out, becoming a safe stairway to the ground below. I jumped the last few feet, not onto the hard painful earth of my fears but onto rich springy turf speckled with tiny white flowers. I immediately looked not around me but backwards up the tree. It hung above my head for a moment, then my senses inverted, and I felt as if I was floating above it, looking towards its roots, which vanished into a dark muddy swirling hole. Disorientated, I blinked, and when I opened my eyes again, the tree had vanished.

I stood alone, upon a windswept grassy plain that extended to the horizon in all directions. All but one, that is, for far away to the presumed east, where the light had welled up, was the grassy mound that I had first seen when the high winds had tugged me around the tree trunk. There was nowhere else to go.

The ground was helpful, which is to say it bounced slightly under me and seemed to push me along. The clear light, the fresh air, the rich grass and tiny flowers combined to invigorate me, until I felt stronger, fitter, cleaner, than I had ever been in my entire sordid, dreary life. I broke into a run and with my eyes fixed upon the distant hill ran and ran and ran until I fell panting onto the ground, which yielded to me like a lover and cradled me like a mother while I sobbed for breath.

Turning onto my back, I discovered that there was no sun to be seen in the sky but a huge array of impossibly large stars, flickering and glinting with many colours. Some were moving with visible speed, and as I looked several bright lights sped across the sky in different directions, leaving coloured trails.

As I lay there stargazing, an increasing feeling of urgency came upon me. I felt as if someone was reminding me, nudging me, whispering that I should make haste towards the hill. I looked around, but saw no one, yet the sense of presence remained until I started to walk again, after which it faded. I was on my way again, pleased to find that the grassy hill was closer now; I walked briskly towards it, determined not to lose my breath or over-exert myself again.

I approached the hill at what seemed to be midday. As there

was no sun in the sky it was difficult to judge, but the light seemed to clarify and intensify hourly, and if I had arrived at dawn I reckoned my arrival at the hill to be around noon.

It was larger than I had expected, a rounded grassy mound. Though it had looked small from a distance it now loomed over me, and I realized that its rounded contour had disguised its true size. It was a huge work; I say 'work' deliberately, for it was artificial, a vast mound raised up long ago, now worn smooth by wind and rain and grown over with grass.

I decided to climb to the top, but felt a curious warning, a voiceless whisper similar to that which had urged me to hurry towards the mound. I looked round, and saw nothing but grass and flowers waving in the wind. No animals, no tall plants, no trees. I looked again for the giant tree by which I had descended and thought that I saw, in the direction from which I had come, a shimmering column of air, water vapour, or rainbow light. When I looked hard the shimmering vanished.

Not knowing what to do, I began to pace around the mound, and as I walked I heard faint sounds like whispers, footfalls, stifled cries. I could see nothing — that is, I saw nothing until, rounding one end of the mound where it narrowed almost to a point, I came upon a stone box. This box was a small chamber, like a gate-house, of stone slabs jutting out of the narrow end of the hill. The wind plucked at my sleeve and seemed to say, 'Now go in there . . .' I spun around quickly, but saw no one. The stone box was sealed with a large square of dark green granite. I pushed upon this crude door and it tilted back, perfectly hinged and balanced. To my shock a man was sitting hunched inside.

I say a man, but really he was not human. His body was thin and tall, and his head was uncomfortably bent in that narrow space. He wore silver and white armour of the most exotic and outlandish kind, covered in spirals and curves and embossed shapes, with exaggerated pointed shoulders terminating in cascading grey plumes. The armour extended only as far as a kilt or tunic might, for his legs were bare, as were his feet. His skin was a pale white colour tinged with faintest rose pink and green mottling. He looked up, and I saw his high cheekbones, slanting violet-coloured eyes, and hair of deep blue with pure silver streaks. He looked at me slowly, with utter indifference, then quickened his gaze towards something behind me and scurried out of the box to allow me entrance. When I stood immobile, he leant within and produced a short spiral-headed javelin made of bone or ivory and gave me a sharp push with its butt.

I fell into the stone box, and the lid swung shut behind me, leaving me in the dark. I heard a muted sound, rather like a polite and formal cough, the type of noise made by a butler or a very discreet head waiter. Then the inner door swung slowly open, admitting a flood of ruby light and my first glimpse of the chamber beyond. 'Go on, you fool,' whispered a voice, 'or they'll shut it again.' So I scuttled through into that red light, and as I entered it transformed suddenly to a vivid gold and green.

The first things that I saw in that place were tall torches fastened, so I thought, to the stone walls. They burned with a brilliant green and gold flame. I looked at the torch nearest to me and found that it was a root, jutting out of the narrow earthen space between two vast slabs of dark green rock. It blazed with green fire, yet was not consumed, and gave off no smoke. Yet there had been no trees above. I took three steps forward, emerging from under a low lintel of stone, and realized how cavernous that chamber was. It stretched away to my right and left as if I had emerged from the middle of one side, though I was sure the entrance had been at the narrowest end of the mound.

There were no magnificent furnishings or heaps of treasure, but a huge bare space, the walls lined with enormous stones fitted tightly together, their unbroken surface showing earth only where the root torches appeared. The brilliant green and golden light illuminated every part of the spacious chamber and cast no shadows. Looking upwards I saw the stone walls taper inward to form the roof, meeting together in a perfect dry seam that ran the full length of that place. The floor of the hall was of polished black slabs, inlaid with fine silver lines in a chaotic disturbing pattern, if pattern it could be rightfully called.

To my left stood rank upon rank of tall warriors with bone-white spiral-headed spears in their long-fingered hands and green metal leaf-bladed swords thrust through their belts. They wore a bewildering variety of strange costumes and headgear: feathered plumes, crests of fishes' spines, animal heads of gold and silver, crystal caps with delicately carved wings, and tall conical bronze helmets inlaid with green, blue and red enamel, and rough, unfacetted gems. Some wore armour like that of the gate-keeper, while others sported quilted jackets and short trews heavily embroidered with abstract designs in subtle colours. A few wore only reptilian-scaled leather loincloths and revealed their tall muscular bodies, their arms and legs wrapped around with heavy massive ornaments in the shape of golden serpents. A small group of these warriors also wore golden serpents coiled around their necks, and these few stood apart from the mass as if superior or in command, their eyes closed in trance, their arms crossed, their legs evenly spaced apart.

To my right I saw a long table with immense stone supports and a surface of flat, highly polished, crystalline rock. Behind this sat a gathering of strangely beautiful men and women in a confusing variety of exotic clothing. Among the many-coloured cloaks, embroidered robes, vivid leather kilts, embossed jackets, concealing and revealing hoods and flimsy tunics, some wore nothing but their tattoos upon navels and breasts, while others simply hung jewels, chains, strings of shells and feathers over delicately pastel-hued irridescent skin. Though both the men and women, or perhaps I should say males and females, for they were not human, had long flowing heads of hair, none had any hair upon their bodies or faces.

In the centre of this group were two tall thrones. One was roughly cut from a huge rock shot through with translucent crystal, seeming to grow long crystalline spurs and clustered outcrops from every jutting corner while its crevices held flashes and veins of varicoloured minerals and metals. The second throne was nothing more nor less than a huge hollowed tree stump, out of which living branches sprouted silver and green leaves. I hesitated to approach this great table, and when I looked upon those who sat within the prodigious thrones I began to shake with emotion. I felt filled with awe, with fear, and yet with profound relief, joy, and ecstasy.

'Stop all that drivelling, and get on up there before they change their minds,' hissed a hard voice in my ear, and I was given a painful blow on the back which made me stagger towards the high table. I looked up into the eyes of the king of that place where he sat upon and within his rock. He alone of the males there grew a beard. Both his beard and hair were long and curling, a rich dark-brown colour with golden strands shining out as if gold had been braided into hair and beard or as if he had stout golden hairs growing within them. His skin was smooth and swarthy, the golden-brown colour and texture of the ripe autumn hazelnut shell. His mouth was firm yet smiling slightly, and his dark black eyes looked upon me, not with the contempt that I had expected, but with amusement.

He wore a simple purple tunic and a long cloak of grey

feathers; his arms and feet were bare, like those of most of the people in that place. In one hand he held a huge iridescent cup, made of glowing multi-coloured shell and set with silver handles. In the other he held a tiny branch made of pure white silver with a golden acorn upon its tip. His nails, I saw, were dark green, almost black, while the hairs upon his hands and arms were white and seemed to move and ripple constantly.

Next to this king, for king he surely was though he wore no crown, sat the most exotic and disturbing female that I have ever seen. Her face haunts me even now, and in that wondrous place she outshone all the other beautiful and strange beings like the full moon outshines a candle flame. Her skin was very pale, and seemed to change colour in slow mobile waves, first a gentle flush of palest green, then a blushing rose pink, a subtle almost invisible violet, then the blue of a wild bird's egg. These colours were so delicate, so subliminal, that it took me some time to realize that they were passing across or through her flesh.

Her hair was very long indeed, reaching over her shoulders and flowing down on either side of her waist, across the rough-hewn arms of the tree-trunk throne with its vibrant leafy shoots and onto the floor. It was of a dark golden-red colour, shot through with black streaks, and like a huge cloak it fell about her. Her nose was long and narrow and her mouth wide, her lips of a curious purple. As the delicate hues of her skin changed, so did the shade of lips, growing paler, then darker, sometimes to red, sometimes black, sometimes blue.

But her eyes were the most remarkable of all. I say remarkable, for no superlative word could describe or evoke them. I looked upon her eyes, for it was impossible to look into them, and was enthralled. They were a tawny golden colour, like those of a hawk, and the pupils were a void bottomless black. About the hollows of her eyesockets she had silver tattoos or patterns within her skin. These spiralled in opposite directions leading off in a delicate tracery across her high cheekbones and down either side of her face.

My eyes must have followed the convoluted pattern of these designs as I rudely gazed upon her, for she suddenly smiled, and the silver line on one side of her exquisite jaw widened and became defined as an image of a serpent. Her teeth, when she smiled, were pure white and perfectly formed, each one being pierced with a tiny clear glowing jewel.

From her smiling mouth, my gaze dropped, not unwillingly,

but certainly in fear, to her body. Her robe was of a leaf-green colour, shot through with many white ribs and veins. Indeed, it might have been a single huge leaf wrapped tightly about her waist and thighs. Her breasts were bare, and there I saw again the serpentine patterns glowing deeply within her shining skin. There was no shame or lewdity to look upon her perfect body, only joy and terror.

I felt the pressure of her gaze upon the top of my head, and slowly looked up again. This time her eyes caught mine, and I was pinned, fixed like a rabbit before the bird of prey. A melodious voice slid through my mind like a razor-sharp, ice-cold, blood-warm, life-devouring blade.

'How short you are. The stature of mortal men has lessened greatly. I doubt if we can use your services here, but perhaps you can take a token back to your people to remind them of us.' And with this she held up a small blue flower, a forget-me-not. It seemed to grow out of the outstretched palm of her hand, appearing from within the skin and then emerging, complete with roots, to slide into her long pale fingers.

I approached the table, and leant over, head bowed, with my hand outstretched. She in turn leaned toward me, and I smelled a perfume of the sap of growing green plants, of rich, warm earth, of honeysuckle, mingled with the cold pure scent of deep spring water. Tears came unwilling to my eyes, and I took the tiny plant, wrapping my hand carefully about it. She took great care not to touch my flesh, and I wondered how *I* might smell to her.

With a tiny movement of her fingers she signed me away from the table, and I stepped blindly back, not caring if I should fall, both regretful and relieved that I need not stand close to her again.

The king then leaned forward and spoke aloud. His voice was the merest thin whisper, yet it ran clearly through that vast hall, and every being in that place raised its head to listen. Their murmuring, which had been as the sea, fell silent. The eyes of the entranced commanding warriors snapped open and glittered like green ice.

'Go back now, little man. I give you safe conduct, and I see besides that you have a trusted ally who attends you. Leave by the same route by which you entered, and do not stray from the path, whatever you might hear or see.'

And with these words, a group of distant musicians struck up a thin eerie sound upon pipes and flutes, while many of the warriors raised wide shallow drums and beat upon them with bones inlaid with wide red stripes. The sound was deep and complex, high and shocking; the interaction between the drums made the floor and walls tremble, while the wailing pipes caused my hair to bristle and my teeth to ache. The company raised tall glasses, bronze and gold goblets, crystalline cups, wooden bowls, and began to drink healths to one another. Suddenly I was ignored, and I stood gaping about me. In that moment of transition, I realized that there were no harps to be heard or seen.

'Move, you slug, before one of the warriors remembers what you are and chooses to hunt you for sport . . . move!' And a pair of invisible cold rough hands grabbed my arm and dragged me away from the royal table.

I reached the low lintel of stone through which I had entered and clambered up three steps into the stone box. As I climbed through the green light seemed to turn a deep cherry red behind me, but when I turned to look back the stone valve slammed shut with a deep boom, cutting off all light and sound from within. The last sight I had of those beings was the beginning of a wild dance. Then moist air flooded through the outer stone door as it opened before me, and I stepped out into an evening light, with a cool wind and shadows seeming to approach from my left. The tall warrior in his exotic silver armour leaned nonchalantly against the stones, picking his nails with a long slim black dagger. He eyed me with hostility and ceasing his manicure reached for the short spiral-headed javelin thrust into his plaited gold-wire belt. But he paused, stepped back, and looked behind me. I turned also, yet could see nothing. As I passed him, thinking at every moment that he might attack, he made the slightest of bows, as if to someone who walked beside me. He ducked back into the gate-chamber and pulled the stone down after him. He seemed to be shaking his head in disbelief or disgust.

I knew for certain now that I had an invisible guide or ally; he or she had spoken to me several times, had pushed me forward toward the royal table, had been mentioned by the king within the mound. Finally my ally had grabbed me by the hands with a cold and rough sensation of scales or perhaps fine chain-metal gloves. But I could still see no one, and somehow felt that he, she or it had withdrawn now that I was back upon the plain at evening. Gently I put the flower, still fresh in my hand, into my shirt-pocket.

The welling shadows approached in pools and streaks, moving swiftly like patches and clouds of fog passing low over the grass. These were outriders, heralds of a high dark wave of seething blackness far to my left. Whereas the region had been empty when I arrived that morning, it was now full of life. Creatures of all sizes scurried quietly away from the streaks of shadow, from the wall of night. They leapt into burrows that I had missed in full daylight, they gathered in groups and ran swiftly away towards a distant forest line, which I was sure had not been visible when I ran so joyfully in the light towards the great mound. I saw rabbits, deer, wild cats, cattle, foxes, many birds in flocks, and other indistinct shapes that stayed out of vision, skirting round me where I stood. The movement of so many creatures had a lulling hypnotic effect upon me, and I drifted into a stillness, a lethargy, waiting for the darkness to envelop me at last.

One solitary figure approached me and paused just beyond arm's length. To my befuddled sight it looked similar to a man, but a man hurriedly designed or made up from poor memory. It shimmered slightly, and I realized that I was looking upon a glamour, an illusion. The sight of it brought me back to my senses, and I began to walk slowly away from it, keeping it in my vision all the while.

'You had best move quickly, mortal man. The Land turns towards the Dark Star, the secret Sun. It is midday in your home place when the Dark Star shines here; a time of terror and doubt. Move quickly, for your ally has departed to go before you and you are alone.'

'What are you?' I asked hurriedly, for I had thought at first that this apparition might be my phantom ally.

'I am a sending from the king within the mound, who reminds you not to leave the path. Go now, for the terror time approaches.'

Even as the shimmering false-man spoke, he fell apart in shreds and was blown away by the night wind. I realized that I stood upon a tiny faintly-glowing slot or deertrack through the grass, and began to move quickly along it, knowing that it would lead me to the great tree.

As I walked, the grass seemed visibly to grow thicker, longer, and pools and coils of shadow slid about within it. I heard distinct high-pitched laughter follow me, and footfalls stamping and rustling, and several times the sound of what could only have been huge creatures mating. The light grew purple and then grey and dim, and the towering wall of shadow seemed very close as I reached the tree.

A single branch-tip touched the surface of the ground, as if the entire inverted tree was anchored by a leaf, and the vast cone of branches vanished into deep indigo obscurity above my head. I prepared to climb.

As I touched the branches, two creatures appeared from out of the shadows, seeming to come from within the tree. They were grey and green, covered with moss and creepers, and each had no face, only a wide flat leaf. They touched me gently with their long tendrils and infused me with a sense of deep peace, the timeless time of growing plants, and perfection of rooting in the earth and reaching slowly but inevitably towards the light. For the first time I understood what it was like to be a tree, a plant, a flower, and I longed to stay with them. Even as I longed, I felt my feet dig into the earth.

In sudden fear I leapt into the branches and began to climb as fast as I could in the growing darkness, pulling myself up by the feel of the branches, not caring if I cut my hands or lashed my face.

I awoke in the middle of a hot afternoon, lying naked upon the floor of my kitchen, with the harp beside me. I staggered to the shower and sluiced the sticky sweat from my body. Dressing quickly I scrabbled for the fourth letter, determined this time to break its cryptic language. Within the envelope, tucked into one corner, was a dried flower.

THE FOURTH LETTER

Oc tiu mixa gaas igja ya ypisjiyu yma fada ac Cixin taa wijj buas cpab paudisb ymin jiyyip. Ic tiu fissuy paid ymin, ymis a ivrafy tia wajj juaps yma ypaym gt neba mapdip biymid. A pis fusnidapgju punkn niyyisb ymin aey cap tae, giy ymi Japdji Asin dinruni yma mabis apy ac wpiyisb in fjubnt isd njuw (wmifm ay in). A duigy ic bmat wejj fisfaps waym ymin, uy guisb usfptryud.

Tiu maxu ifqaiped a caupt mipr. Taa fussay nijj iy yi asta-sa, isd taa fus isjt bixu ay yi asu wma ankn cap iy nruficefajjt, wmifm, gijiixu ba, in a cap jinn jiikajt affipasfu ymus tii babmy ymisk. Iy in rjais, ymiabm sey wiymiay nkijj in fpacnybasnmir, iy nuubn yi afqaipu a ryesa ic bpibu xupt qaifkjt, an ic nuekisb yi midu iynujc . . . ip rupmarn iap wipjd in yii ciaj cip iy yi pubais pubais fjuas. Hast ruirju apu nagyjt saenuayud gt iyn rpunusfu, ymiabm a cuw cisd iy ippunyenyigjt canfisayisb, asd ymupecipu annabu ymay tia, ymu iwsup, wijj suxup repy wiym iy. Ni ymut di siy ank cip iy, ymiabm ymut jisb yi maxu iy.

Ymu isjt wat yi gu cpuu ic ymen igjibayiis in yi puyaps ymu mapr yi ymu jasd ic caipt. Ymupe apu hast watn is asd iay, asd hast yuppigje usfiasyupn is ymey rjafe. Biid jafk.

Isu jany cafy ymay tia nmeajd ksiw in ymin; ymu mapr gpisbn wiym iy, ay fupyais yihun, a fihrasiis ip fi-wajkup. I suypuay tia, an tia xajau tiap jicu, yi afksewjdbu ymin fi-wajkup, wmayexup nmaru iy yakun wmus ey cisejjt arrapn yi tia. Ymut fas gu nyaasfm ajjiun, gay yuppigju ihrjafagju ciun ic ymut apu asayyesud.

Tiapn is giym wepjdn,

A Cpeusd.

RIDE THE WIND'S BACK

This tale is also a fiction written in the first person. That person is not necessarily myself, but most of the setting for the tale, the people in it, the city described, are, or were, real. A disturbing magical song has been set within a contemporary visionary tale, or perhaps the tale finally emerged from the song, which originally appeared in my mind in the late 1970s.

I would say that this story crosses the obscure border line between a true magical tale and the modern genre of the horror story; it uses imagery from an ancient and potent theme, that of the Dark Goddess of Sovereignty who destroys to preserve and regenerate, yet occurs in a contemporary world rather than a mythic or alternative one. It does not, however, employ any of the sillier devices of modern horror stories such as rotten corpses, sexually rampant demons, wriggling worms from the grave and so on. These images are, after all, merely immature and hardly worthy of serious consideration in a world replete with true horror.

But the contemporary world described in 'Ride the Wind's Back' is not exactly identical to our own in terms of recent history; as far as I know no nuclear disaster has occurred at Berkeley on Severn, though it is mentioned along with that of Chernobyl as an aside by our narrator. The enigmatic medieval *Prophecies of Merlin*,[20] state that in the late twentieth or early twenty-first century the River Severn shall burn, and breed monstrous fish. Prophecies are not fixed realities, however, and only serve to suggest potential events and forms, arising from forces which are perceived by the seer when his or her imagination flies ahead of the illusion of serial time and causation.

Traditionally prophets are the conscience of the people, instilling a sense of responsibility through visions of potential futures.

No such hopeful suggestion of potentiality can dispose of the terrible vision in this tale, however, which is a global one, and already familiar to us all.

Tarot images

Despite the ambience of horror to 'Ride the Wind's Back' it touches upon subjects and perceptions or realizations which are central to magical arts and to serious spiritual development and insight. We can employ a tarot sequence inherent in this tale as a vehicle for personal insight; meditation upon the patterns shown in Figure Two will bring many disturbing but catalytic or cathartic realizations into one's personal failings, illusions, weaknesses. True magic is intensely involved in such transformative insights, far more than with golden radiances of holiness, sweetness, or undeserved benefit from superior entities. The images are as follows:

1. The Knight of Cups/Warrior of Fishes (or any Court card to represent the narrator, who is yourself)
2. Death (a female figure in *The Merlin Tarot*)
3. Judgement
4. The Blasted Tower
5. The Ten of Swords/Ten of Birds
6. The Ace of Rods/Dragons

These cards form a triangle of Trumps around the Court card chosen to represent the personality, with the Ten and the Ace forming two poles or pillars on either side of the Blasted Tower, as shown in Figure Two.

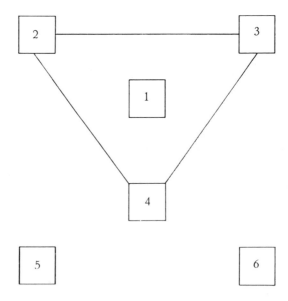

Figure Two: The Insight Pattern

RIDE THE WIND'S BACK

Historic places draw people to them . . . not just the wealthy or the tourists, but lost, dismal, displaced people who have come because of the name, the rumour of an easier time on the streets, the climate, the atmosphere. Certain cities seem to mysteriously specialize in eccentric vagrant men and women; the place where I live is one of those. I should say immediately that I do not count the sturdy beggars . . . the van people, the self-styled 'New Age gypsies' who are neither of the New Age (yet to come, reckoning by even the most enthusiastic calculations; if, indeed, we are here to see it) nor of the blood of gypsies, who are a genuine nomadic race with their own traditions. The van people have muscled in, not upon the gypsies who rightly despise them as frauds, but upon the vagrants, the really displaced lost ends of society, depriving them of their few havens, and generating such public hostility through aggressive begging that the true down-and-outs suffer even more, pushed even beyond the lowest ebb that they had reached in years gone by.

As time has passed, there are more and more sturdy beggars and less of the shy, untuned, strange people on the streets. I can think of old Jock, who had missing fingers, playing upon the harmonica to earn pennies, and when sober intelligently discussing the declining state of Britain. Or the mad Pole, who slept in the abbey doorway and would queue quietly each day among the blue-rinsed ladies in a very genteel delicatessen, he seeming as offended by them as they were by him, to buy a fragment of sausage which, presumably, reminded him of home. He could not speak a word of English, communicating by signs and grunts. He died one winter night of the bitter cold.

Women too crept about the streets, often drunk like Jock's girlfriend ('See here, big fella, this's ma girlfriend'), a lady in her fifties whose name I never heard, with her sailor's hat and rubber-jawed wrinkled face, looking like Popeye in an old cartoon. Sometimes the ladies talked to invisible people, twittered and cooed to the pigeons, collected bags of rubbish and wheeled battered prams.

I miss those people; I used to sit with them, talk to them occasionally on warm days, and sometimes give them money . . . but when we knew one another they would never ask for favours or beg from me, but instead offered me the opportunity to share their luridly-coloured wine, or perhaps a stale sandwich. As my house is in the very centre of the city, they were my neighbours.

Now the aggressive, disgusting New Agers have driven them out, or perhaps I am mistaken and they are all dead. Time blurs out the memory of street people, and I suppose we try to erase them from our minds to ease our conscience.

One encounter, however, remains with me in detail, clear and bright. I cannot see a television news report without remembering it, but to say this is to anticipate the story.

During my frequent walks about the city, being something of a fresh air fanatic, though the place is notorious for its dull tepid atmosphere through most of the year, I had seen a small hunched figure wheeling a pram. She, for I presumed it was a woman, always wore a dark green raincoat, tightly wrapped about her with a long length of rope, the hood pulled over her head, even on the hottest summer days. She had stuffed both her coat sleeves and pram with old wrapping paper, plastic bags, rubbish from cast-off shop displays dumped in the back streets. Indeed, my own street is one such back alley, where the traders do not hesitate to throw out their rubbish indiscriminately at any time of the week. Being a fresh air fanatic, as I have said, I slept with the windows wide open when the weather was dry, and occasionally heard, three storeys below, the squeak of wheels in the middle of the night, then the rustling of papers and an indistinct muttering, rising and falling in pitch, almost verging upon song.

It seemed that she did not sleep, for on my early morning walks, when it was possible to find clean air and fresh winds before the rush-hour traffic jams began and the tourists appeared, there she would be. Or there she would not be, for I always saw her just turning a corner heading away from me, or in the distance silhouetted against the rising light on a wide Georgian avenue. Her stuffed sleeves leaked plastic film or paper, making her look like a mobile scarecrow or Guy Fawkes dummy, ready for burning in celebration of 5 November, the gunpowder plot, or the even older November fire festival of Samhain and the rising of the Pleiades which marked the turning of the year for our ancestors.

Sometimes I would hear the rattle and squeak of wheels close by, for the centre of the city is full of tiny intersecting alley-ways, where in the stillness of night or early morning you can hear people before you see them. Yet, turning a corner, there would be no one in sight, merely the echo of wheels further off, or a scrap of polythene tumbling along in the gutter.

After a number of such non-encounters, and her occasional visits to my street at night, I suppose I began to become a little obsessed with this bag lady. I wanted to meet her face to face. But she was clearly shy, like many street people, and I thought that if I leapt from my door and confronted her in the middle of the night she might flee in terror or even have a fit, collapsing inconveniently upon my doorstep. So I tried, unsuccessfully, to catch up with her during the day. I even asked Jock and some of his Scottish friends, countrymen of mine sharing English exile, if they knew about her, but they all denied ever having seen her.

Their denial was odd, for they were usually only too happy to tell their own and each other's life stories once they were accustomed to me sitting upon their bench in the abbey square in the sun, even though I politely fended off their shared drink. I must state at this point that I am not a missionary, an evangelist, or a social worker; maybe that's why they accepted me so easily. We were neighbours, after all.

It had been, in both local environmental and global terms, a very bad year. An oil tanker had devastated yet another stretch of coastline by sinking and spilling its cargo; another ship filled with toxic waste had leaked into the English Channel; rain forest was vanishing at an incomprehensible rate to create beef for hamburger bars throughout Europe and America; nuclear waste had been leaking from certain very safe installations into the sea and the atmosphere; while many terrible religious and political wars were supported by devious means in impoverished lands. And that, of course, was only the news that we were allowed to hear. At that time we did not know about the depleted ozone layer, and the chemical disaster of Bhopal, and the nuclear explosions at Chernobyl and Berkeley on Severn were yet to come.

'This country's gaen tae the dogs', said Jock one relatively sober day. 'See, the time was that ye could travel aboot in peace, and get a kip in the Sally Army hostel, or on a bench in the park, nae bother. Now ye canna do that, what with the polis moving yous on and the streets . . . my god! They're so bloody filthy a man canna sleep oot in them . . . pollution, that's the world's biggest problem, you mark my words, big fella, pollution and dirt will finish us all off before too long. Nae bother tae me, mind, I'll be long gone by then . . . God, this used tae be a great country tae live in . . . look at it now, would ye?'

I don't suppose that I worried endlessly about the environment, though I prided myself on being more aware of the problems than the so-called average man or woman; in truth I never understood what was happening at all, so when I met the old woman face to face I was totally unprepared. Now of course, I remember her whenever I see a news report on television, or a newspaper headline, but we are all much more aware nowadays . . . we have to be, don't we?

Very early one midsummer morning I arose, and set out for my walk. The air was cool and fresh, the sun bright and the sky clear. Birds sang pleasantly, there was very little traffic. The formal city gardens leading down to the river were clear of litter for the moment, full of neat patterned blooms, and the entire place was revealed with a sharpness, a clarity, that made my own perception brilliant, alert. It was going to be a good day, I thought, as I strode manfully down the empty road. I felt fit, relaxed, alive, even carefree. Perhaps . . . well, who knew what could occur on a summer day so promising and fine?

As I turned the corner onto the bridge, a sharp blind corner as it happens, where people often bump into one another during the busy tourist-filled day, when one cannot step out into the road for fear of traffic, I saw her coming down the empty street towards me. The bag lady, the pram person, the grubber among rubbish, the midnight wheel-squeaking collector of empty papers and discarded wrappers. The maze of the city had finally brought us together at one time in one place.

I slowed my pace, thinking to say good morning, but she had already stopped, seeming oblivious to my presence. She bent low over her pram and rearranged newspapers carefully, lovingly, as if they were of considerable value. One double page fluttered away in the morning breeze, and whipped past my face quickly. I caught the words 'Greenhouse effect' on the headline as it passed.

Then I heard her singing softly to herself, strangely sweet and clear, as she somehow rearranged the papers within her sleeves, both hands hidden from sight, her head bent over, her face unseen within the ragged, blackened hood.

At first there were no words, simply a lilted melody; it seemed as if the song was aimed at me for a brief moment, and I thought of autistic children who occasionally communicate through music, rhyming slang, or other oblique methods. While this frantic rationalization skipped through my brain, the words of her song exploded into a sequence of bright terrible images:

As I went out walking, walking,
For to view the morning fair,
I overheard a woman talking,
Talking to the empty air.

Oh empty air and wind a-blowing,
Hear my words and sing my song,
Long time now I've been forgotten,
Long time now my love is gone.

Long time now the oak tree withers,
Long time now no small birds sing,
Long time now he never passes,
Touching all the lands with spring.

Blow me a flame to light a fire,
Blow again to burn it bright,
Blow a blast to blaze a forest,
Blow the stars out of the night.

There's some who spend their time in laughing,
Some who spend their time in play,
I will bring the time of passing,
I will take their time away

I am she who rides the wind's back,
I am she who calls the storm
She I am who calls the whirlwind,
From its distant distant home . . .

Each verse, each line, hit me like a hard blow in the face, the words, the chant, the terrifying images. As the last verse finished, she began to lilt and hum again, and turned towards me, lifting up her head.

It was not until that strange fluid movement that I realized that I had never seen her hands; not while rearranging her papers, both arms tucked into one another, or pushing her pram along with her body; even as her face rose to confront mine, I wondered how she could have rummaged among the rubbish in my street without . . .

Within the hood was a small, deeply wrinkled face, barely the size of a child's face, or perhaps that of a woman so old that she had reverted to the most basic meagre substance. She had a hooked nose and downturned mouth. Her eyes were shut, yet she looked directly at me, and for a moment I wondered if she was blind. Then her eyelids snapped open, revealing orbs of blank pale blue, washed with high white clouds, like windows directly into the upper sky. I instinctively ducked and put my arm over my face. That was what saved my own sight, I suppose, though my hair was singed and my sleeve and arm burned.

'Vandals in arson scare', said the local paper; after I had run from the bridge and fumbled my way back home, the police and fire brigade had been alerted by a passing delivery truck, and had dealt with a burning pram, once full of old rubbish, mysteriously set alight on the bridge at dawn. People were warned against leaving rubbish out where it could be fired by vandals.

How could I have reported it to the authorities? Ah, excuse me officer, but an old woman, or something that I thought might have been an old woman, exploded into white flame in front of me . . . no, they would have thought me insane, and probably booked me for arson. No human remains were found, only charred fragments of metal pram, badly melted, and fine paper ash. My own slightly burned arm and hair healed quickly enough, though I did not seek medical care. I had fallen flat after covering my face . . . not because I expected a blast of white instantaneous fire, but because the brief sight of her eyes had terrified me into that position. Her eyes, and the realization that she could not have been human.

My fear may have saved me, but every time I see a news report on the television, or read a paper, I remember her song, the clear hard images, and the knowledge that she had burnt into my unwilling mind. We can no longer rape and destroy the planet at will, nor is it simply a matter of our own greed and folly coming back at us in terms of self-imposed destruction and pollution.

She, whosoever she may be, has raised the fire, called the whirlwind, and like the hostile entities which we are, we are to be excised, purified, wiped out. We are the enemies of the planet, and a new force will arise, has arisen already, to dispose of us utterly. What form that force will take, I cannot say, though certain possibilities spring easily to mind.

Why she chose to appear to me is another enigma; I'm not the prophetic type, and prefer to hide away quietly. Perhaps she knew that; perhaps seeding the knowledge of her presence, her summoning, into one human mind is enough, and from there it will percolate through to us all . . . too late, of course. It was too late when I saw her, and it has taken me ten years to be able to write these words.

RETURN

No collection of magical tales would be acceptable unless it contained something concerning Merlin, about whom so much trivial nonsense has been written that his original nature has been obscured in the modern imagination. [21]

In 'Return' a detailed magical ritual is described; this is not a fictitious ritual, but a re-enactment of one of the great traditional rituals of Western magic. Whereas in most so-called 'occult' text books such a ceremony would involve long-winded invocations and gradiose speeches, Merlin conducts it all without uttering a word in any known language, and hardly any sound at all until he is inspired with a potent verse. Towards the end of the tale he feels, deep within his mind, a short line form a liturgy which is known today to members of a specific magical order. [2] Thus the entire pattern of the ritual consists of movements, symbols, glyphs or circuits of power around the magical circle, transformations of shape, signs, colours, and resulting visions. It transcends or cuts across time and space, for Merlin seeks to rescue the souls of dead soldiers who obviously come from a war far in his own future, and paradoxically they cannot yet have been born.

Although this is a story concerning magical ritual of the type once — and still — native to Britain, described by the medieval chroniclers as 'necromancy', though we today would call it more accurately ancestral magic, it also touches upon spiritual themes. The aim of Merlin's strange ritual is to make a bridge through into the worlds of light, the spiritual dimensions of existence that are central to the great religions of our world, regardless of variant forms and images dictated by dogma. It need hardly be said that all magical arts, all imaginative or inner disciplines, all transformations, realizations, individuations and initiations are worthless nonsense unless they continually move towards spiritual enlightenment.

Finally a word of warning: Merlin was able to conduct the ritual successfully.

RETURN

One night in November, when the seven stars of the Pleiades were closely watched and hallowed gates stood ready to open, the prophet Merlin sat awake in his observatory tower. Scattered about him were the implements of his art . . . a rough fragment of brown stone upon which white crystals grew; a small apple branch twisted into a loop, where the parent tree had grown over a hidden spring; a simple wooden bowl filled with red well water; a hooked sickle of polished golden bronze.

The prophet had watched stars crawl within the layers of night, seeing within the sky-shadows each fold of the Lady's Shawl, each curve and twist of her weaving. He had followed the racing Moon as she sped to encompass all nocturnal events before dawn; he had marked where star rays touched upon certain power places, signalling potential futures of mortal men. Yet he felt incomplete.

The night before the hallows were revealed, before the portals opened, yet Merlin felt unready. He could not sense a quality or action required for completion, or discern in which of the Four Directions it might be found. Below his tower a thick mist rolled about the hilltop, creeping to a shadow daybreak. In one hour the time of inner knowledge would pass him by.

What had he missed? What had he forgotten? The prophet picked up his apple branch and touched it lightly to the crystalline rock; his awareness reached down, far within the earth below the hill, and he spoke the names of two dragons. But he met only that utter silence which falls upon all kingdoms awaiting dawn.

Putting aside his ritual objects, each charged with power, Merlin took three paces to the east of his circular stone chamber; three to the south. He turned next to face north, taking six paces across the centre of the circle to its northern wall; finally he turned to his left and took three steady paces west. The mist outside thickened and slowly curled and twisted, writhing and rising until it covered the tower, seeping through unprotected deep slit windows built for star-watching by daylight. Finally the prophet faced east once more, and took three paces to the centre of his chamber.

He felt not that the mist was rising, but that the tower was plummeting down into the rocky hill below; it seemed to sink like a stone dropped into a well shaft. For a moment the stout elm boards beneath his feet seemed to ready to fall away and leave him floating. Merlin turned to face north once more, pivoting upon the central point, stamping upon the floor and squinting hard at the rough, unadorned stone wall before him.

At first he saw nothing, heard nothing. Only the jagged surfaces and planes of the blue lias stone, cut long ago by craftsmen, shaped and laid to make the tower, a long familiar pattern of surfaces, lines and shadows in the lamplight. But still seeing nothing, he suddenly heard something.

From beyond the north came a hint of sound, then a certain murmuring. The murmuring grew into droning, and the droning became a growling which swelled suddenly into a roaring, until Merlin realized that knowledge of incompletion and completion awaited him in the north, just beyond the thick wall of his downward-plummeting tower.

Yet, being not only a prophet but a bard and (at one time) a madman, he chose merely to wait and listen to the terrible sound that swelled and rose and expanded out of the wall. In that raging storm he could hear voices calling to one another over great distances, speaking in the tongue of a time and place far beyond his own. Certain voices were filled with pain and fear, others uttered firm, dry, hard commands. The sense of great distance would suddenly snap tight and short, until the crying, screaming, ordering voices were packed close together; they would then disperse and echo down long tunnels, and, as if a tide washed them to and fro, they would suddenly regroup within the eye of the sound-storm and scream at one another through its throbbing violence.

Listening, waiting, the prophet gained his first hint towards completion. This was, he realized at last, a convocation of warriors lost in a terrible conflict, wandering spirits of men killed in a far distant war, distant in time if not in space. Those who died thus, sadly and suddenly, were unable to break free from the shadow world into the worlds of light.

He also realized that this was no mere essay in far-seeing or coincidence of imagination; here was a matter of great import, and the vacuum which he had felt before the sound-storm, his sense of being empty and incomplete, had been a vital forerunner and preparation, a low ebb before strong turning of the tide towards flood.

Yet he remained still, standing, filling his spirit with deep silence to absorb the sound; he awaited a sign to enfold the moment, to direct him. As he stood utterly still, facing north in the centre of the circular chamber, a tiny spider scuttled over his bare feet and ran off into the darkness behind him. She had fallen from a small gap between the dry-laid, tight-fitting stones of the northern wall, disturbed by the roaring and the voices. She ran directly to the south, where all was quiet; the sign.

So it was that Merlin raised his arms above his head to summon up and open the secret gateway of the North. There had been times in the wildwood, the cavern, in the ancient places filled with power and terror, which had strengthened him for this task. First he took the name and form of Bear, strong guardian of the icy northern realms. His shoulders grew broad and slumped forward, his arms massive and heavy; his face grew long and keen and claws ripped open through his hands and feet. His eyesight dimmed greatly, but his hearing and sense of smell were amplified; a great heart beat soundly in his body and he began to turn and weave in motion, sniffing out each quarter of the circle as he moved.

Dancing the shuffling Bear dance he drew the strength, courage and motion of the bear into his hands, then passed it right into the northern wall, sealing it with a shape of power known only to those of the Bear lineage. The prophet then spread his arms out straight at shoulder height, level right and left, lowering them from the upraised position. He turned completely around, moving in the pattern known as the Door, spinning for an instant upon one foot, so fast that he seemed to have two heads. The shape of Bear passed from him, but the power of Door flowed out of him into the northern wall, and he sealed it with a colour of power known only to those who are Doorkeepers.

Merlin lowered his arms from their horizontal position, until both hands pointed down to the chamber floor and to the earth below the tower. His fingers shook and his skin pulsed with the flow of power, reaching far down into the core of the planet; slowly he began to raise his arms again, slowly and greatly laden, bearing a burden of rising force without form. As his rigid trembling hands reached out before him, drawing level with his shoulders, he turned his wrists in the supple undulating pattern of Opening.

As the Opening was born, he uttered an ascending musical call that crept from the depths of earth, low and grinding at first, then crystalline and deep, then swelling waves of ocean, and roar of trees meeting wind. Within that call were all the undertones and overtones of music through the Three Worlds. Suddenly it

rose into the heights, and twisted into the high triumphant
scream of the hawk flying into sunlight in the month of May.
And with this sound, known only to those who are Merlin, he
sealed the Opening into the northern wall.

Pausing to take stock of his work, as do all experienced
labourers who rest before they tire rather than when fatigue
weakens their strength, Merlin looked upon the wall. It was still
an ordinary stone wall, in every respect the same as it had been
before he commenced his work but for one difference. In the
centre of the wall a door had appeared, made of dark oak boards
under a low arch. Upon this door was carved the image of a
dancing bear, and the handle of the door was enmeshed in a
looping heavy blue chain that shimmered coldly in the shadows
of the room.

Beyond this door the prophet could sense the presence of
another time . . . he understood now that the curling mist had
come from out of that time, and that within its clouds men were
dead or dying, lost, broken, far from home. Violent sounds of
screaming, shrill metal under stress, muffled roaring, tense
shrieking of war engines unknown in his own time assailed
Merlin's hearing as he stood facing north.

Here was a decision of some weight: how should these lost
souls be passed from world to world, how would they find their
way home; where, indeed, was their true home? Reaching within
himself Merlin took counsel as he had learned to do. For a
moment nothing came and he seemed empty, poised over an
abyss of silence, void of all being. Then a tight and potent verse
arose complete within him; it came alive somewhere in his belly
and rose up to fire his breast with inspiration; it pumped his
lungs and burst forth into his eyes; it set his head aflame with
light and seethed into the outer air. The words that came were
reflections, echoes, of its inner potency:

> I sit upon a high place
> On hard rock;
> I look upon a land,
> Ring of broken bells
> Song of flown bird,
> Anger of dead place,
> Murmur of lost people.
>
> No mere love may ease them

No drug appease their pain,
No sleep heal such wounds.

Not I with my sight
Or harp of hands,
Not plucking strings
Not singing back daylight,
Nor I in the broken tree
The empty nut
Star clouded
On the drawing waiting height.

Nor you, a single child,
Nor any child of blood
Can open terror's eye,
Pluck forth the root
Then stem the deep born giant of the flood.

Up stone and under reach
In earth the warm veins leach
Out dark gold from waiting suns
Into web-ways for your gift.
Friend's hand alone shall shape
The drowsy stone
Becoming joy to heal.

Distant is the time of which I speak,
Open is the heart on that wild day
To all pain, all voices of the weak,
All victims of the wheel.

Yet distant is come close
Upon this hilltop chair;
There is no moment of unwoven space
I may not touch,
No measure of unspiralled time
You may not share.

As Merlin uttered these words of power, he felt himself dissolve
or reflect into countless images, mirrored within one another
through an endless tunnel. When the first sound of the last word
began, he felt the long-awaited response behind him in the

south. Beyond his line of sight, behind his back, a great gate had opened into the worlds of light. Within that gate stood beings unknown to the human race, yet compassionate.

With the last letter of the last word, Merlin shattered the three bonds upon the door in the north; the Shape, the Colour, the Sound. The blue chain melted like ice, the Bear symbol faded, the door became dull unmoving wood. Then it split apart, exploding with the force of conflict in that place beyond. The dark opening filled with orange flames, flashing lights, and ghastly momentary visions of a land utterly ruined.

Merlin gazed calmly upon the doorway until the first human shape appeared. It was a young man, rubbing his hand across his eyes as if he could not believe what he was seeing. He took a tentative step into the chamber, and Merlin saw his strange clothing of dull green and brown, his wooden and iron club held backwards, pointing before him, the narrow black handle outwards and the broad wooden striking blade tucked into his side. The young man's hair was grotesquely unnatural and short, his belts and straps were hung with small metal objects and amulets, their purpose obscure and sinister. One leg was ripped and bleeding, and for a moment the prophet almost reached out to take the wounded warrior in his arms and comfort him, but he knew that this one was the first of many. No mere comfort would suffice.

Within the shattered doorway they assembled, hardly daring at first to pass through, then slowly gathering momentum as if compelled by the many massing behind. Each seemed to reform as he passed through, his shadow becoming substantial. Not one looked upon Merlin, as if the prophet was unseen or unreal to them.

As the terrible pressure of their passage increased, Merlin bowed his head and closed his eyes, anchoring himself within the memory of his own true time and place. He felt the unseen southern gate behind him drawing in the spirits of these strange warriors, and did not dare to turn and look upon their translation.

Like a rising gale they flowed past and over and through him still clutching the redundant weapons of their world, still wearing their ugly garments. What they saw within the south Merlin could not assess. He knew that it was a vast multifold realm of light, within which all elements were transmuted by that power known to him as the Dragons. He knew that it took many forms in many worlds, and that truth lay within and yet beyond them all.

The long night progressed, and with the dawn the last of the warriors had passed through the gate of the south. His shoulders slumped now and his body aching, Merlin looked upon the open door in the north. As he looked he became aware, with the last ebb of his exhausted perception, that some further terrible power lay just beyond that war-torn horizon, some mystery that he dared not fathom in his exhausted state. He thought of his own prophecies, uttered while still a child, and knew that the answer lay somewhere within them, but was not for this night.

Behind his back he felt the bright resonance of the worlds of light expand momentarily to touch him, then snap shut. Deep within his mind he felt the words, 'I am a Light and a Keeper of Lights . . .' the closing line of the ritual of the Doorkeeper uttered by the higher being that overshadowed him. The northern wall blurred and resolved itself into simple stone at last. Merlin closed the circle with the Four Signs of Peace, and gently washed his trembling hands in the bowl of mineral red water. As the song of birds reached into the tower chamber, he stretched out upon his simple bed and slept.

THE GAME OF CHESS

The traditional magical ballad 'Tam Lin' forms the basis for this tale, and one version of the text for the song is found in Appendix One. There are long and more complex variants of the ballad, which was known to singers in Scotland and America, and has several European parallels; the verses printed here are a typical terse version from Scottish oral tradition.

'Tam Lin' centres upon a multifold theme, or a knot of themes that cannot be fully undone or cut through. It seems, initially, to relate to fairy traditions, in which a human is captured by the Queen of Fairy, and his true love releases him by a ritual at the crossroads. This level of meaning, however, is possibly the last or uppermost of many levels, reaching far back into ancient myth and ritual. Rather than attempt yet another analysis of the ballad, I chose to focus upon a retelling of the tale.

As is often the case, certain apparently minor elements leapt forward demanding attention, mainly 'The Game of Chess'. In the original narrative, four and twenty ladies gay are playing at the chess, and in comes the fair young Janet as pale as any glass. What was a poetic device, pehaps, suddenly becomes a major focus for the tale. Furthermore, when Janet retrieves Tam Lin from the grasp of the Otherworld, she also puts an end to the Game. It is not, however, chess as we know it in this world today.

As in the original ballad, it is not clear in this story whether Janet is rescuing her lover, or actually giving birth to him as a child; the sequence of mysterious lover, pregnancy, and magical birth is found in most myths and religions, and need not be elaborated upon here.

Modern interpretations of the traditional tale of Tam Lin have dwelt at great length upon his sequence of transformations, likening them, rightly, to alchemical changes, to the seasons and months of the years, and to the shamanistic or magical changes undertaken by initiates into the old primal Mysteries. Personally I do not think that there is a 'complete' or 'correct' sequence of transformations: there are different transformations for each individual, though most changes partake of a general sequence rooted in the interaction between humanity and the environment, represented by many myths, legends, and specific magical practices. In this story, therefore, the changes undergone by Tam Lin are, intentionally, not clearly defined, though they do seem to connect to the mysteries of gestation and childbirth.

The vessels for water and milk which stand at the crossroads (see Figure Three) are derived from actual ritual vessels, long-preserved at many sites. Few of these remain today, though examples may be found in prehistoric sites in Ireland. In the nineteenth century, local people told Sir Walter Scott (though his testimony must always be taken with a certain amount of caution, as he fabricated a great deal to suit himself) that the fairy rings found in his locality were the actual site of Janet's ritual reclamation of Tam Lin into the human world. Whatever the validity of this, we do know that 'fairy rings', or zones of rich growth are found at certain ancient sites; in Scotland, offerings of fresh milk were poured regularly upon such spots as tokens of regard or perhaps propitiation to the fairy folk. Little wonder, a cynic might say, that the grass grows so greenly upon such sites, with such a tradition of enrichment of the soil.

The Fairy Queen in this tale is not a glittering little sprite with a shining wand; she is, in fact, the Great Queen or Phantom Queen, *Morrighan*,[17] a terrifying goddess of the pagan Celts, acknowledged even by materialist psychology as a dark constituent of our consciousness.[15] General literature on Western spiritual and magical traditions has tended to lose sight of such potent female figures, though they are well preserved in Eastern traditions to this day, and have always played a major role in the true practical working magical and mystical arts of the West.

Yet the Dark Goddess is, despite long efforts to purge her from the imagination, well-known in early literature, legend, myth, and inscription in the West and her suppression is, of course, a matter of Christian history. Her revival, however, is not a matter of cozy pseudo-paganism. She is a potent, demolishing and empowering force in nature and within ourselves; no true spiritual development or magical initiation may occur without her double-edged blessing.[1]

She appears in tradition, and in this tale in triple form, though not necessarily in the well-publicized triplications found in modern literature. In 'Tam Lin' certain well-described images are used for the Fairy Queen, who appears, or rather utters curses without actually being seen in person, towards the close of the ballad. Three of these, allocated to three of the Four Directions, are found in this tale. They are, in short, key images of the Great Goddess in her dark or destructive aspect: black crows flying over white ice; a flowering broom plant (*Sarothamnus scoparius*) within a cloud of fire; and the cry of an owl within which is the voice of a young girl. Needless to say, these are not images to be worked with lightly or superficially; the imaginative forces aroused by this sequence may be balanced according to the Four Directions, just as they are in the dramatization of the story itself.

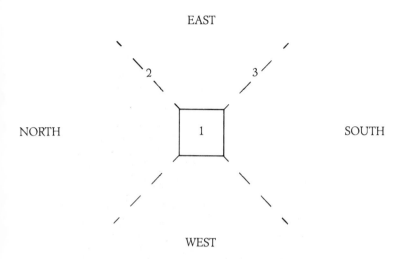

Figure Three: The Cross Roads 1) Standing Stone Cross 2) Vessel of Milk 3) Vessel of Water

THE GAME OF CHESS

It was the chess tournament: twenty-four women, in twelve games, playing against one another. The winner of each game would progress about the great square gold and greenstone table being herself a transforming game piece in a pattern. The final role, of course, was that of Queen. Each square of the table was in itself a board, either green inlaid with alternate silver squares, or gold inlaid with alternate black squares. The inner boards were played by using long, finely-carved ivory wands to move each piece, though skilled players could move their pieces by other means.

Janet leaned over the cold stone balustrade and looked down upon the game below, six women to each of the four sides of the huge game table, and the squares flashing brilliant colours in the morning sunlight. She felt sick, as she had for several mornings

past. Each crystalline chess-man uttered a fine ringing sound as it was touched by the wand of a player, and a constant flow of assonant tones filled the great room, echoing back from the domed ceiling far above. The high clear tones and the flashing colours made her even more nauseous, and she was glad that she had not been selected to play this year, even though her playing would have been a courtesy matter only, she being the high king's daughter.

As she stepped back from the balustrade, about to return to her chamber and wait for the nausea to pass, she felt a deep pulling sensation within her. It was as if some innermost part of her body was being drawn away, and must drag the rest with it, or be torn out. She knew that upon the hill someone was blowing a horn, and felt in her deep dress pocket for the withered rose. A thorn stabbed into her thumb and drew blood, and as she sucked the blood away to ease her pain, the pulling started again.

Upon the great game table below, pieces began to vibrate suddenly, causing the players to look about in alarm. Clearly the distant horn was reaching even the crystal pieces: the men at arms, warriors, maidens, the deadman, and the queen, upon each board. Janet withdrew quickly before she could be seen.

From her room a small stone stair led down into a back court-yard, and through the courtyard door she darted, out into open country beyond. It was not a long walk to the little wood upon the hill which her father had given to her, but before she reached the outermost trees, the silent horn blew again, tearing at her innards. She ran into the low thorny bushes, the wild roses that had been her special gift, and on under the hazel trees. Towards the centre of the wood was a bubbling spring, where, she knew, someone awaited her.

Pausing, panting for breath, she leaned against a hawthorn tree close to the clear pool. He was here, she was certain, but could not be seen. Three times he had blown his horn to summon her, yet was further off now than he had ever been.

When they had first met he had appeared suddenly beside her, a solid handsome man, with dark curling hair and deep brown eyes. She had plucked her first rose of the spring that day, rejoicing that her father had given her this rose- and hazel-wood as her own special place, perhaps with some good magic in it. But with her tearing of rose from branch, the young man had stepped out of the bushes suddenly, with no sound of rustling branches or snapping twigs. He had been angry, too, demanding by what right she pulled flowers for her hat in this hallowed place. But she had laughed, and told him that her father owned all the land around, and had given her the little hill for her very own wild pleasure garden.

What had happened next was a mystery, for the handsome young man seemed to blur and shimmer, dissolving into a golden cloud, humming like bees upon a hot summer day; while she herself felt drowsy yet seething with unsatiable savage desire. When she woke she was in her own bed at home, with the pleasant morning light shining through the long tapestry that hung over the deep window. She thought it had all been a dream. Until the morning sickness.

So she had gone to the wood again, to find that small grey herb which old women talked about in whispers, and again the man had appeared, or rather his voice had come to her out of a thick tangled mass of wild roses, woodbine, and hazel. This time he had told her his name, Tam Lin, and that he was guardian of the wood, set to watch the spring and the rose bushes by the queen of the land. Janet had not believed this, for her own father ruled hereabouts, but in the confusion of his voice from the bushes, and the sudden warmth that she felt for him, even though he remained unseen, she forgot to pull the abortificant.

And now he had summoned her with a terrible unrelenting summons, drawing upon the child in her womb by some means that she could not understand. At the centre of the wood, by the clear pool, she waited for him to speak. This time his voice was very faint, as if travelling a great distance, yet it was right by her ear, as if he also stood beside her and whispered gently.

Now he told her that he was a prisoner of the Great Queen, and that she and her terrible people intended to sacrifice him at the November feast, when the gates between the living and the dead stood open for a brief wild moment. Janet pitied him then, and pitying him she remembered that she loved him, as if it was something that she had always known but had superficially forgotten while busy with the trivia of her entire life to this very moment in time and space.

Three times she had met him, and each time he had been further from her. Three times he had blown his horn to summon her and now he was furthest away, yet closer and dearer than ever. She listened well to the instructions that he offered, and when his voice finally faded, and only the sounds of the wood could be heard through the rising wind, she quietly went home to wait for the festival in November.

But by that time, of course, her belly was swelling, and her father had long since found her out, and challenged her to name her lover. Her obstinate refusal enraged him, and he swore that she would be married to whatever half-decent warrior or chieftain might have her, bastard and all. After all, she was a high king's daughter, as much as anyone could tell, and he could sweeten her pregnancy with many gifts.

Janet refused to consider such an outrageous idea, and no matter how much her father shouted and raged, disturbing the chess players below the gallery where he and she stood jutchinned and hands on hips arguing, she refused to be married. It was her right to choose her own husband, just as it was her blood that carried the royal lineage, and not his. Such pretensions from a man, father, king!

The king pulled his plaited, silk-ribboned orange beard, and slapped himself in the face several times, turning purple with rage. The he stamped off to muck out the pigsty, which was, of course, the royal prerogative. The chess game settled down again, and one tall, calm lady moved her queen with an elaborate flourish of her fingers. The piece glided swiftly across the central board to check mate the deadman. The adjudicators beat upon their huge bronze gongs until the royal hall vibrated in every stone. Dust seeped out of tiny cracks in the roof, abandoned game pieces fell over on their boards, and as the reverberation died, nobody dared tell the king that he was about to be married again. But of course, the pigs had already told him, and it did not improve his temper in the slightest.

The November festival came not long after the royal marriage that year, so many of the wedding games ran on into those for the turning of the winter stars. But no one could hide the tension as the turning time approached: there were many dead friends, relatives, enemies, to consider, and always there were unspoken questions about the year to come.

So in the very centre pit of night, when beans had been cast, fires raked through, milk poured, and much wine and beer drunk, everyone lay snoring or trembling in their sleeping chambers or on the rushes upon the chess-hall floor. Janet, however, was wide-awake, and creeping towards the back courtyard gate.

She carried, with difficulty, a great skin bag full of fresh milk, which she herself had taken from the huge vat of that day's milking, declaring that she wanted it to bathe in. It was heavy, and made loud gurgling and deep slapping sounds, as if to announce itself to all and sundry wherever she passed. She had never realized that milk was so noisy.

Beyond the gate she had tethered a quiet donkey, who patiently allowed her to sling the grumbling milk across its back, and walked by her side towards the dark wood upon the distant hill.

The night was very still indeed, as if all sounds had been terminated. The stars were small and clear. On this night the terrible armies and hosts of the Otherworld were said to ride, yet all was peaceful. Janet felt suddenly cheated by the silence, and then relief replaced her fear. Perhaps nothing bad would happen at all, she thought to herself.

As Janet, the donkey, and the grumbling milk crept through the dark meadow towards the trees, they felt a deep vibration in the damp earth beneath. It was as if a host of riders passed through the ground far below them, the hooves muffled by the clay, yet distinct enough to recognize even individual horses. But within a few moments the sound had dwindled into the distance. Janet increased her pace, so the donkey added its complaint in concert with the milk. They reached the border of the wood, where the first few stunted bushes reached out of blackest shadows, but instead of striking into the trees, she took a faint path around the woodland, towards the high crossroads beyond. Again she felt the host pass through the earth beneath her, the sounds were louder now, as if they neared the surface, and even a faint sound of voices could be heard, crying in a high strange language.

Now the donkey brayed and tried to bolt. She coaxed his ears with tickling and breathing, and he plodded on, leaving the woodland behind, and coming out onto the high bones of the downland. As they moved so slowly through the cold night towards the open crossroads, Janet realized that the rumbling beneath the earth had first travelled from behind her and then from her right. It was as if the unseen host of riders had travelled south to north, and then east to west. She could not understand this at all, and used the puzzle to suppress her growing fear. There was no logical answer to this problem, she decided, and, seeking further distraction from terror, listened instead to the milk. It seemed to be saying:

First I was green
But now I am white
First I was warm,
Now I freeze in the night . . .

This gloomy message helped her not at all. She laid her hands upon the great leather bag, and it drew the warmth out of them. Deep inside her, her baby suddenly kicked, then became still.

Four ancient upland roads met together at a high flat place, and there Janet, donkey, milk, and baby, stopped. She quickly lowered the bag of milk from the donkey's back, and he stood trembling with fear. At the very centre of the crossroads a tall menhir rose up towards the stars, and upon it a thoughtful missionary had carved the figure of a small man with a teardrop-shaped head, his arms spread out wide in the shape of a cross. She doubted very much if this religious emblem would protect her, but gently touched it out of respect for all victims upon the Wheel, no matter what name or origin. As she did so, a faint flow of energy seemed to emanate from the figure, as if it moved slightly beneath the warmth of her touch. Again the baby in her womb kicked then settled peacefully.

The milk had stopped complaining as soon as it was set upon the ground, and Janet looked about her for the stone basins. There they were, overgrown with long grass, unused for many years. Two deeply etched bowls, each big enough to hold a human. In the cold, under the faintest starlight, she pulled the grasses away, and scraped the bowls clean, using a bundle of long grass and ferns to make a thorough job of it. She could feel the spiral patterns in the stone, but could hardly see them. Into one bowl she poured the milk, which made such a loud noise as it poured that the donkey bolted off into the dark, his small hooves tapping lightly, speedily, upon the stones of the road.

Now she felt the need for haste, for the middle of the night must be drawing near. Using the empty skin, she drew water from the traveller's well at the foot of the menhir, and filled the second basin. As the water reached the brim, dark clouds seethed overhead, and suddenly she could see nothing. In the distance, coming it seemed down all four roads, and upon the very surface of the earth, she could hear a host of riders. The bridle bells rang, shrill bird-like voices called and cried, harnesses jingled, and the ground began to shake at their coming.

Then four great hosts, one from each corner of the land, drew near to the crossroads, and in the total darkness Janet knew that she would fail, for she could see nothing. Cowering behind the tall stone, she realized that she could not tell any difference between the black, brown, and white horses as her lover had bidden her. He would be riding on the milk-white steed, after the first black and the first brown horse to reach the crossroads. But all horses are black in the dark.

The host surrounded her with a great roaring and pounding and ringing; she heard their long lance-heads clashing and for the first time smelt the heady perfume of their kind, making her head spin and wild sensations flow through her body. Then she felt again that terrible pull from within. So strongly it came that she was jerked out of hiding in the shadow beneath the stone like a helpless puppet, her muscles working despite her will. The blackness was lit by flashes of white and green and gold, shimmering outlines of wild figures with long flowing hair and violet eyes; a wildfire flowed over and around and through the great host that milled and merged about the cross, seeking a new direction for their charge. And the white horse shone like a star, like a mirror reflecting the dawn, like love within a maiden's eyes as she lies with her first man. Upon it he rode, with a tall, spiralling, crystal crown upon his head and blank unseeing eyes. Just as he had bidden, in full defiance of the host, she leapt upon him and dragged him to the ground.

Instantly the riders formed a great circle about her, galloping and screaming, forming a blur of colours and sound. She lay panting upon the still form of the man, seeing the shards of the crown glitter upon the rough stones all about. Then she felt his shape begin to change.

His body elongated beneath her, his hair lengthened and coarsened and the rank smell of a wild beast came from him. Rippling muscles sought to shake her off, and a gust of hot, meat-rotten air roared out his fanged lion's mouth. But she held onto him gently as if the vicious beast raging beneath was her own baby, and suddenly the lion shape sagged and melted. The host fell silent, circling her with a hissing of indrawn breath, faster and faster yet, until the ground trembled only slightly, as if they passed above it in their spinning. She did not lift her eyes off the ground, knowing that she must not yet look at whatever she held, nor at the circling riders.

But as the riders gained speed, so did the transformations. She felt an amorphous sea beast, a lithe dry serpent, a clicking hook-jawed insect that rasped its legs against her face, tearing her skin, a flapping bird with a harsh beak and claws, other shapes and smells and sensations followed one after another, each trying its uttermost to throw her off and away from out of the shadow of the protecting stone, out under the hooves of the circling host.

Then the transformations paused, and she felt heat. Her eyes were tightly closed; she felt the shape beneath her become rigid like metal. Hot metal; the burning calor of it seared her hands, singed her eyebrows away, and she could smell the burning of flesh and hair. With a great burst of strength, she flung the burning metal into the bowl of well water, and a cloud of steam shot up high into the night.

The circling host stopped dead, horses staggering into one another and spearheads clashed and tangled. Still the water seethed and boiled as something struggled within the ancient basin to gain shape. The stone seemed to glow with heat, and in that dim light she saw what might be a hand, glowing amber with flickering blue veins and red bones showing clearly through it. She crawled to the basin, and pulled herself upright, defiantly gazing upon the vast multitide that watched now in stillness and silence. Reaching in, she lifted the glowing man-shape firmly, grasping it beneath each armpit, and with a scream threw it over into the basin of fresh milk. Instantly the milk began to talk; it babbled with voices that she knew, her mother and her mother's mother, both dead, her long-buried aunts, her murdered sisters, all entreating her to take this terrible man-shape away before it destroyed them and cast them into the shadows with its golden heat. Then the milk slowly turned blood-red, first in streaks, then in broad clots, then into widening veins. As it turned to blood it fell silent, but the man-shape within beat its arms and legs, thrashing about until it fell out onto the grass. A beautiful naked man, unconscious. She wrapped her long green mantle about him, cradling him in her arms, wrapping him until not one part of him from head to toe could be seen.

The clouds above rolled back as if a great wind had snatched at them, and the cold clear light of a full moon shone into the circle. Suddenly she was aware of the army surrounding her, the rainbow-coloured eyes of the horses, the purple glowing stare of the riders, the deadly long lances. But as one the horses fell to their knees and the riders flung down their weapons and covered their fair, terrible faces with their hair. Janet assumed, for a giddy instant, that they made obeisance out of respect for her courage.

But out of the north came a grating cry like that of a night bird, and with its sound the horses flattened themselves upon the ground, and the riders shook with terror. The Great Queen had come.

Janet sat still as still, exhausted. She saw the terror of the riders but could not comprehend it. What person, what force, what power could bring such a host to its knees? Then, slowly, the circle of abject horses and riders parted, making a narrow gap, straight as an arrow toward the north road. Janet saw nothing, but felt in the furthest distance, as if beyond the northernmost North, the wheeling of a flock of black birds over ancient ice; the voice of a crow seemed to reach towards her and pass through her as if she was nothing, for it sought the man that she cradled in her arms, and had no other purpose but to reach him. It asked him how he had allowed a mere human to steal him back. But he slept, protected by Janet's mantle, warm and at peace.

Then the crow voice withdrew, and the prostrated army shuffled and reordered, the riders wrapping their long white hair ever tighter about their faces and moaning softly. An avenue opened to the south, and beyond the southernmost horizon Janet thought she saw a bush of green broom in full blossom, yet raging with consuming fire. From out of that bush came a warm, loving, and deadly whisper: the Great Queen called upon her two sister-selves to witness this impudent theft of a life from her realm to that of mortal men. The golden murmur sunk into the ear of the sleeping man, but still he heard nothing.

When the voice died Janet began to wonder how they might fetch home to her father's hall, and knew that she would not be allowed to pass unscathed. Within the circle of the crossroads and beneath the guardian stone she was, briefly, safe, but she dare not step beyond the limit of the basins of milk and water. As she thought of this, she looked upon the basin that had held the water, and saw that it was dry. Next she looked upon the basin that had once held milk, now turned to blood. As she looked the blood in that great basin seemed to drain away, as if taken in drink by an unseen presence. Then the eldritch army moaned and writhed and fell from their horses and covered their ears with their hands, pushing their faces into the horses' flanks to further muffle their hearing.

And from out of the west came the cry of a night owl, and within that the voice of a young girl. And again the voices passed through her towards the sleeping man: they sobbed and hooted and lilted that if they had known of such treachery as love, they would have plucked out his soft gentle brown eyes, and put in eyes from the knotty trunk of a hawthorn tree. And had they known of the power of the mortal heart, they would have torn his living heart from his body, and replaced it with a heart of granite stone.

And then the flock of crows, the burning flowering bush and the owl maiden rose up together and stretched their power toward the centre of the circle. The elfin horses screamed aloud, a tearing, desperate sound, and ran mad, kicking at their masters, and biting each other in the necks until clear green ichor flowed over the grass, which began to move and grow wherever the fluid touched.

The tall standing stone, with its tiny carving of the man, his arms outstretched in blessing, began to vibrate with the power of the Great Queen. Janet bent her head over the sleeper in her arms, and knew that when the stone shattered they would both die, at best, or at worst remain alive. She prayed for death, even if it was death for herself that he might stay alive and go free.

And with her prayer came a sudden hush, and the presence of the Great Queen faltered then snapped away suddenly. Janet remained still, her eyes tight shut, awaiting the next onslaught. She could no longer hear the screaming of demented horses or the terrified fairy warriors. But there came instead a faint chorus of birds in the distant wood behind her, heralding the light of dawn, passing down the eastern road towards her.

When Janet and Tam Lin returned to her father's hall that morning, they found a new chess game about to begin. The king, with an unusual display of good sense, named Tam Lin his tanist or successor, and ambled off to talk to the pigs.

Janet thought awhile, then took it upon herself to secretly remove the queen pieces from each of the boards, at night, one at a time. Of course no one suspected her, and no one has solved the problem of how to play the game properly from that day to this.

The Woman of the Birds

R.J. Stewart

Introduction

In 1980 I was snowed into my apartment in Bath for three days
(unlikely as this may sound) and a sheet of ice effectively sealed
the door to the street. Under such primal conditions, I found
myself writing the basis of a multifold novel, which I was to
develop over the following six months, in which five themes interlinked in a very devious and complicated manner. Needless to
say my agent at that time (long since gone the way of most agents)
shrank back in terror at the thought of placing such a monstrosity
with a publisher. Such are the vagaries of a writer's life...but
superficially simple situations hide complex subterranean rum-
blings.

The original novel consists of five visions or worlds inextricably woven together. During my work on the manuscript I saw these worlds, entered into them in inner vision, and interpreted what I saw in my own language. One such world, that of 'The Woman of the Birds', seems to be in the prehistoric past... readers with a good knowledge of British geography and prehistory may recognize the locations, though it took me several weeks to do so myself.

The two scenes which I have chosen are part of a coherent tale, which makes a full novel in its own right, though I would prefer it not to be separated from its four companion stories. For the present anthology, however, these scenes are offered as insights into primal or tribal magical arts, retold from my vision. I would stress that this appeared to me in every way as a real world, with real people, and that their plight moved me very deeply, for they were dying out. The scenes, however, deal with two magical themes or aspects of oral tradition and initiatory knowledge. The first is concerned with what would nowadays be called genetics, but genetics for magical or spiritual ends. I have been told by a geneticist that the 'code' described in the communal chant of the birds is perfectly viable in modern scientific terms, but I merely take his word for this.

The second scene is a tale within a tale, and deals with the much vaunted, little understood subject of relationship between matriarchal and patriarchal cultures in the distant past. The story develops as a myth told to a group of children, but it includes an account of the deadly art of cursing, a number of highly energized visionary symbols, such as were later to be formalized in tarot, and a version of one of the most famous myths found world-wide in so many forms, the 'Massacre of the Innocents'. Many of the elements of this second scene, such as the Spider and Weaver Goddess, were to appear some years later in my *Merlin Tarot* (1988) as emblems or symbols in the cards, drawn primarily from Merlin texts and traditions written out and adapted by Geoffrey of Monmouth during the twelfth century. But in 1980, shivering in my winter woollens, I had not yet read the *Life and Prophecies of Merlin* and had not yet written my books on these curious texts.

The Woman of the Birds

The Woman of the Birds sat uneasily upon her High Chair. This chair was large, made of many animal horns twisted and tied together with thongs; it was crowned with two immense curving long-horns rising in a crescent far above her tiny head. The creature that once wore those horns no longer walked in the land. Perched upon a mound of skins and furs, the Woman of the Birds shifted uncomfortably from side to side. She was the smallest of a long line of small women, and old and wizened. Most of her people towered over her, yet her word was absolute law. In the Wooden House, smoke and shadows danced from flames that burnt pungent herbs; in that shifting light the women who gathered for the evening chant loomed as silent wavering giants against the reed-lined walls.

Within the smoky warmth there was security of hearth and home, but outside winter gripped tight upon the marshland. That very morning she had stood upon the wooden roof platform, newly cleared of snow, to peer out over the flat white land into the grey wall of mist and cloud that hid the sea. The log causeway to the West was covered with thick, hard ice, and snow upon that ice, so even the lightest runners could not travel between her settlement and the hilltop fort that guarded the route inland from the sea. On clear days, when the fort was in full sight, mirror and fire signals could travel back and forth in their own languages; mirror for women in tongue of mirror, and fire and smoke for men. Today. . . nothing. Dull grey snowlight hid the road, the edges of the marsh, and the distant fort.

As the Woman of the Birds relived her look-out of that morning, the last of her women entered the chamber, drawing the doors tightly shut against the bitter wind. There were rustlings, soft breathings, the sound of bare feet in rushes as they put their wrappings into a small side-room. No one spoke. All waited for the little creature on the High Chair to signal a beginning. Still she moved restlessly, lost for a moment in an inward dialogue, in memory pictures. Why was she so uneasy? No warriors would seek to travel in such foul weather. . . no raiders could sail; so why be concerned about the guardian fort? She told herself that there was a strangeness about, a strangeness that prickled upon her innermost thoughts, remaining withdrawn and unclear, as if she had seen something in the morning mist yet forgotten its importance. That family vision, inherited from her mother and mother's mother, which came often in time of need, was strangely silent. When she used her Sight upon this mystery that troubled her, she saw nothing. The disturbance came from a different source, from a place where Sight could not reach; it made itself felt as an awareness that whistled and twittered during the most quiet moments, withdrawing instantly whenever she looked directly for its source. Recollecting herself and her time and place, the Woman of the Birds raised her chin slightly and nodded into the smoky light of the hall.

Instantly the great bronze gongs boomed and rumbled, and the high voices of her women opened out into song. They uttered a wandering air, each word elided into the next until any part of the chant seemed to offer many simultaneous word patterns. For the listener the effect was entrancing, confusing, for it relaxed the normal lines of verbal logic and opened the mind directly for waking dream images... and for subtle power-words that held multifold meanings. In certain men this chant produced a fit, with frothing at the mouth, jerking of the arms and legs, and then a huge energetic flinging backwards of the body. Such men, it was rumoured around the evening fire when women told quiet stories of the past, had been used physically in bygone days. No one knew the truth of this tradition, first whispered in girlhood training, at bath time or in the sweat chamber, then repeated in old age with other fragments of the past. But in the present men prone to falling fits were rare, and all men were excluded at all times from the chanting, so there seemed little ground for the suggestive tale.

Herbs and resins were added to the central fire, which was kept burning day and night all year round, save for one night in which it was allowed to die prior to the Mystery of its rekindling. Though the hall grew dark with smoke, no one coughed or paused in the chant. Of those who sat and sang, each knew her own level of chant, according to her age and skill. Some had been singing for as long as 30 years or more, while a few of the youngest girls merely hummed parts of the melody, being just old enough to begin speaking.

On the Horn Chair, she who led the people, men and women both in all aspects and patterns of life, was silent. Silence was her right; she alone was exempt from the rule of chanting, whereby all women must learn the sacred songs as soon as they begin to speak. Her silence stemmed from total knowledge of all chants in the world, all words possessed by the people since the first opening of the eye of the Moon. It was said, by those who told the tales of men and their ritual use in times gone by, that if a girl could not sing and learn the words of power, she should be impaled (as was the rule once long ago). But a woman who could not sing was impossible, unthinkable, so no such rule could be enforced, even if it did truly exist.

The Woman was old, and had both led and listened to this evening chant, the most powerful and secret of all, for more than 50 winters. This was long indeed for one of her people to live; she knew each word, each doubled and seemingly accidental syllable and musical inflexion, each phase of inspiration and interacting resonance. She knew every image that arose within the chant, always the same images forever. Sometimes, alone at night, and greatly daring, she had speculated upon this chant, seeking out its mystery which none had fathomed. . .for no one understood its meaning and purpose now. Faint echoes of meaning sometimes came to her, preserved within the dream of the tradition, but whatever sacred knowledge those perfect words and tones contained was lost to her, and certainly lost to her people.

Not first there is man. . .of the seed.
There is also woman. . .of the blood.
Man of seed, woman of blood.

Man of seed comes from blood and blood:
There is also man of blood.
Man of blood is from woman-blood
Once joined with not-blood.
Woman-blood and not-blood.

Woman of blood comes from blood and blood:
There is always woman of blood.
Woman of blood also comes from blood and not-blood:
There is always woman of blood.

Not last comes one of seed-blood
From woman of blood and man of seed:
In right time of turning
Comes one of seed-blood.

Woman has the line of blood
Woman has the mystery of blood
Woman ends the exile by her blood
By mystery of blood and seed:
Woman has the line of blood.

Man has one chance of blood
Man has one chance of seed
Man has one given chance.

Woman has the line of blood
The line of blood all ways:
Woman gives the blood to man
Woman is the branch forever:
Woman ends exile by her blood
By mystery of blood and seed.

Not first there is man...of the seed.
There is also woman...of the blood.
Man of seed, woman of blood:
In right time of turning
Comes one of seed-blood...

As the chant repeated, her mind relaxed into that half-sleep that comes with great age, resting yet in part alert. She knew many chants, yes...chants for the growing of corn and of nut trees; chants for the homing of bees to their hives; chants for the summoning of black birds in autumn; chants for the rising of shoals of fish in the river pools; chants for the making and birthing of babes. They all had clear meaning but for one, this first chant learned before speech, this last chant she would hear one evening soon.

In her dreaming memory the chant led her back upon her childhood journey, a tradition that had long since ceased with the lessening of the people and the closing of the sea-ways. She had travelled with a small party of other girls of her age, led by an aged woman who had also commanded the sailors. They had rowed and then sailed to the South and West, to a group of islands far away in the racing sea. There lived the furthest families and rulers of her race, not led by Bird Women as in her homeland, but by Man Kings. These curious male Bird Women had spirals pricked out painfully around their eye sockets, dyed in rich blue-black and purple. Some were patterned around one eye, some around both, some even had balancing spirals upon their cheeks; they met the girls and immediately pointed to the patterns upon their wind-brown faces...this is the Pattern of the Eye.

In strange lilting accents they claimed to see into anyone's most secret heart through this pattern, and although her cousins were doubtful, she knew this to be true. For a thin brown man (they were all kings, each and every one of them), had sat her upon his knee, given her a fruit to eat, told her wonderful stories, and sung the secret evening chant of the women to her. Then he predicted her entire life. He told her of the Horned Chair, leadership, responsibility, pain, joy and great age. Before he finished the tale she had fallen asleep.

On returning home she had told this wonder to her elder cousin, the senior woman of the group who was destined to be Woman of the Birds when her mother's mother's sister, the current Woman, died. The older woman, already preparing to rule, had been surprised and offended.

Those weird Island Men...know more than a man should. In our settlement any man even listening to the great chant has his globes cut off and is cast out into the marsh! This had puzzled the little Bird girl for a long time, she not knowing what a man's globes might be. Even when she found out all about men, their globes, and the uses that men might be put to over and above being herders, runners, sailors and musicians, she never saw one castrated and cast out to die. During her time the community was so small that no one would have wasted a man, no, not even the most conservative and easily offended Bird Woman, such as her elder cousin had never become. Ah! That slim young runner from the fortress men; what endurance and sweet breath. Ah! That fine man who had made the voice within the wood speak out, the song of the hollow tree branch and the fine beaten wires of red metal. Her head nodded, and the evening chant washed over and through her dream.

If any woman noticed that she slept within the shadows, none dared to comment. Besides, none could stop the chant with its numbered repetitions, until all variants were completed. Each woman was enwrapped utterly in the flow, the resonance, the rhythm, sometimes breaking into high subtle ululation. This call marked the bloodline of the Bird Woman, even to the lightest degree. Occasionally the bronze gongs roared, cutting through the flow of the chant and creating complex counter resonances with the voices. And still she slept beneath the powerful high spreading Horns.

The Woman of the Birds tells a Tale

The upturned faces were attentive, the gathering was quiet. Once in each year, when the Seven Stars were seen to mark the onset of fine weather and sailing time, the children were taught by the Woman herself. This was a great event. Each solemn small face was scrubbed clean; best woollen clothes had been patched and whitened with clay or bleached in the sun. Sitting in a wide semicircle at a respectful distance from the High Chair of Horns, the children hardly dared to breathe; any that wriggled or coughed were instantly jabbed by the hard elbows of their neighbours, or smothered in restraining affectionate grips. No adult was present other than the Woman herself.

Sunlight radiated through the open vents in the steep roof, and the sound of birds singing was clear. Already the swallows were beginning to build their nests; the Woman of the Birds could sense them flitting in and out of the swallow-gates at either end of the Hall, even though they could not be seen. The tiny ornately carved archways would not be closed until the last birds were seen to fly off into the unknown at the end of summer, when the ships came home and the Seven Stars began to move towards the place of winter.

Looking at the little ones she realized with no surprise that there were less this year than last. It had been so for several years. But one time, one fine year long ago, this Hall had been filled with children, and many of them male! Why, she had been young and healthy then, and three (or was it four?) of them had been of her own blood and body. Today there were 30 or 40, perhaps a few more, and it was unlucky to count them lest such daring brought further losses and misfortunes. Her chairwomen counted sacks, counted sheaves and jars, stones, even single beans . . . but nobody counted people, not even the Woman of the Birds herself sitting upon the Horn Chair.

As she considered these waiting children, she realized that they must think her very fierce and stern, glaring at them in silence from her immense throne. She smiled to soften their judgement of her, to relax them ready for her lesson. What should she teach them upon this day of days? It would set the tone for all the lessons that followed until winter, for the children would retell it to their teachers, who would draw upon their vast sources of tradition to elaborate endlessly and introduce skills and examples into the telling and the learning. Her mind moved back to her own childhood, in this same Hall, listening hard to a very stern Mother give her annual lesson at springtime. There had been the story of the cow that never ran dry; the meaning of the heron's call; the naming of the trees which told of how they gathered on the highest hilltop to catch their names as the moon emptied out her travelling sack, and each had to catch a name before the sun rose or be nameless forever. But she had told the tree story only last year, and now the children knew the name and function of every tree to be found in the land...though these were few enough.

It was required that the Woman of the Birds tell a different wisdom tale every year for each of the eight years that any one child would appear before her. Musing upon this, she knew that although there were many stories, each child would only be able to hear eight, and that it was difficult to remember which tales had been told in any mixed age-group of children, and to ensure that no child heard any tale twice. Her mind trembled upon the edge of most daring calculation...until a small movement caught her attention, directly in front of her left eye.

Shining in the sunlight, descending from a high beam, a small spider busily spun her way to earth. Her long lifeline glistened, and the warm light made her waving legs and bright body glow like crystal. Just below the Woman's nose, she paused and turned slowly, slowly, in a full circle as her line was caressed by an unfelt wind. Grasping tight for an instant, the spider waited, then released her grip to continue spinning her journey to the hard-packed earthen floor. There, thought the Woman, am I; a long frail line from the unseen to the final earth.

'Today you will hear of the truth. Hear and remember, that the truth will never fade away.'

'We hear and remember, Mother of All.'

'Today, under the blessing of our roof, under the shining of the Sun, upon the foundation of the earth, you will hear of...The Spider.'

'We will hear and remember, Mother of All.'

'So let the story and its telling now begin.'

This ritual opening over, she leaned forward smiling, and summoned them close with her hands. For a moment they hesitated, unsure, surprised, but the first few jumped up and boldly ran right to the foot of the Chair, and the rest soon followed. With the sound of bare feet upon earth she heard little laughs and mutterings, for the sudden release from that respectful sitting had given them the chance to make a sound...to risk that wl ch was usually forbidden in her presence.

So few! She wanted them close. Close so that her voice could be easily heard by all, close so that they felt warm and crowded together, brothers and sisters all, as it had been in the better years long gone when children packed the Hall from the Chair to the Door. But most of all she wanted them close for their own sake, and for her own, almost forgotten, long-dead loved ones. Waiting while they settled, she watched the older children hold the hands of the little ones who could hardly speak, or who might wander off, fall asleep, or lose full attention to the story. She saw those nearest to her feet look carefully for the travelling spider before sitting down. Very few of her people, young or old, failed to see and mark the path of a spider. And then she began...

'A very long time past, when the world was smaller and stronger than it is today, this land was sister to another land. The other land was really a group of islands, which are little lands that stand upon the surface of great heaving waters, far over the seas from here, in the direction of the sun at evening, where he goes to sleep. At the time of this story, a great ruler had arisen who strove mightily to unite all lands under one strong arm; this arm was, of course, his own. Such ruling of lands by one person, and a man at that, was not a good thing. With his loud booming voice and his black curly beard, he rode upon a horse, something which was unknown before his time. The horse carried him to many distant places, with his male guards and male weapon-people running and leaping and stumbling along behind.

'When this man upon the horse reached the sea, and could not ride or run or swim, he caused a great wooden ship to be built. This ship was held together by thick twisted hide ropes and hard wooden and copper pins, and it had many oars, so many that no one could count them, even if they had been allowed to by the vigilant male guards with their bull-whips and clubs. So great in size was this ship that even the horse could ride upon it, standing in the prow just as boldly as he might stand upon the grassy earth.

'This mighty male ruler, with his hard hands and leather armour over his thick skin, forced all the wise women and seeing men to obey him and him only. Those who did not obey he killed, as easily as if they were marsh chickens. There was no end to his ruling, his power, his name and his glory. The Sun shone down upon him and into him, making him glow hot. Soon he would rule all beneath the wide summer sky.

'But take heed, for power is never given without the seed of its own destruction hidden in its heart. Through each season of riding, ship travel and conquest, this man of sinewy arms and broad shoulders knew little rest or sleep. No, not even in the gentle dark night with women close by, not even at the right and proper times for resting could he rest. And it was not the passion or the fire of his power that kept him wide awake, even though his eyes hurt and his mouth tasted of sand, even though his shoulders sagged and his muscles twitched with fatigue. No. . . it was the power of a curse!

'Now a curse is no small thing to make, and no small thing to be the victim of. As soon as it is made it grows and feeds; first upon air, until it begins to seek. As it seeks it travels with the wind for company, and so feeds deeply until it finds. With every spiteful thought and evil deed seen by the wind, a curse will feed, growing strong and heavy, tough and tangled. Until, at last, it finds the one for whom it was made! Some curses find their man or woman quickly, others take many years. A really well-made curse will take a long, long time to hit its mark, for the maker knows that it has grown slowly to become a curse of immense power and cunning, not easily endured or shaken off or destroyed. Such was the kind of curse put upon this bold and mighty self-appointed king, and this was why he could not sleep, for he feared it drawing close upon him.

'Listen now to the story of how he earned that terrible curse, and what came to pass after the curse had been made.

'One hot summer day, while sailing from island to island, with his horse standing proud in the prow of the great ship, just as if it stood on dry land, the ruler of men espied a little mark upon the surface of the sea. As they travelled on, he soon saw that it was a small boat of skins bobbing over the bright wave-tops without oars or sails. In this round frail coracle was a wise man from an island, who had the Seeing Eye in deepest blue upon his own eye and upon his face. This wise man, a type of male Bird Woman now long gone and almost forgotten in the world, was not, as you might think, running away.

'No, for just as a traveller in our straight marsh roads sees first the tree-top then the whole tree as she draws closer and closer to the woods, so had this wise island-man seen the ears of the horse sticking up over the wave crests. As soon as he had seen those ears pricking out over the watery hills, he knew that he must set foot within his skin boat. Even as he pushed his way out into the sea-road, he could see the horse's eyes peeping over the weed-strewn waters, and then the gleaming top of its proud head. He knew that if he was to make a good strong curse, he must be off his own island and out into the open ocean before he could see that horse's nose!

'And this he did, for when his round leather basket, held tight across by one rough wooden sapling pole, floated up to the great ship, his homeland was far, far behind. The great self-appointed king looked down upon his visitor, who looked back up at the king with deeply-spiralling eyes, right at the broad hairy face of the invader.

"There's some who spend their time in laughing!" said the man in the little boat.

"There's some who spend their time in play!" said the king in the great ship.

"I will bring the time of passing" said the one with spiralling eyes, and even the horse laughed at this unlikely threat.

"And I will take *your* time away!" yelled the invader as he hurled a great studded and spiked club right at the island man's head. But as is often the way with the sea, his great ship rising up and the little leather boat bobbing down, the club missed its mark, and tore through the skins of the bottom of the boat. As it began to fill and sink, the island Bird Man stood upon the sapling that spread the leather tight. He perched upon one foot, with one eye shut, and one hand raised.

"Cursed are they that would ruin a fair land" he said out of the left side of his mouth, "And as this boat is filling up with sea faster than the sea fills up with boat, I'll leave out the rest. But I will tell you this much...exactly nine moons from the day that you dare to set foot upon my island, one will be born who will be the death of you and all your works in years to come. Goodbye."

'And with these words his mouth was filled with sea, then his nose, and his eyes, until the salt waters closed over the top of his head. Not once did he struggle, or flap his arms, or shout, or even sneeze; Nor did he try to swim away below the water. And this sort of death is the strongest way of birthing a curse that a man or woman may ever contrive.

'So the great invader, enraged by the challenge, took all the islands. He ruined and burned the island of the Drowned Man, and set foot and feet all over it until nothing was left. He then returned home to the mainland, to a certain place not far from where we are sitting today. But as he sat idle, he began to fear that curse, and so he had all the men who had rowed his ship put to death, lest they spread the tale of it far and wide. Still he could not sleep, for after their needless deaths those dead men rushed upon the wind and on the backs of flying geese to feed the curse, and join with it in revenge. Oh sorry man to have dared what even a woman would not dare! The only living witness left of that cursing was the horse, who never spoke a word, and who enjoyed riding around upon a ship and clopper-ing over the hard roads with a great warrior king upon his back. So the horse was not likely to tell anyone of the curse, and he lived on.

'As each Moon came up from out of the earth and grew, as each Moon faded and closed her eye upon the acts of women, this false king grew to dread the fruit of that sea-made curse. It was indeed a great curse greatly shaped; a curse of curses. He knew that it would last for many generations, working its way through the bloodlines of the first-born carrier, always seek-ing to destroy his works, his hollow-reed empire that was to last forever. And he wished that he had never seen the sky over that island man's head.

'By the eighth Moon, the false king had concluded that there was only one answer, one way to steal sleep. This answer was so simple, so daring, and so horrible that none but a great leader such as himself, so he thought, would dare to carry it out. His solution was this. . .all children born around the period of that ninth Moon would be carried off and executed, which means killed.

'He laid his plans well and set spies through all the corners of his realm to watch. When the ninth Moon opened her all-seeing eye and walked upon the sky-ways to illuminate the land, he sent out his warrior men, with hair standing up straight in hard clay-stiffened spikes. Each new-born child, they announced, was to be taken for counting by the great king's Chair Women. But the secret plan was not counting at all, but killing. When all those tiny babes were gathered into one place, the warrior men whipped out their sharp brown knives and cut them to pieces! The blood flowed into the earth at that place until the earth could take no more, and even to this day there is not a tree, a bush, or a blade of grass that will grow there.

'But this awful deed was that false king's undoing, and was in itself the first effect of the powerful curse against him. It turned all the women of the land into his enemies, and they spat upon the floors where he had walked and ground sharp points upon the ends of their distaffs. No man dared eat food prepared by a woman, and all the secret herbs that breed death were gathered in until no more could be found, for they were all making their way into the food of the great false king and his spike-haired warrior men. Yet this was only the merest beginning of the power of that curse. Listen again and you shall hear who defeated the strongest of men, and she only small and weak!

'In one village there lived a quiet, peaceful woman who had just given birth. Her own story is one that you shall hear upon another telling, but at this time she lived in an old hut, with heavy wooden doorposts; as is the sensible custom the animals lived in with her through the cold winter nights, and they all roamed free in summer. Every morning this woman would take a nutshell and draw pure water from a holy well that rose in a cleft rock just behind her house. She would place the nutshell full of water deep within a large crack in the left-hand door pillar. And who was it for? It was for her who lived within that left-hand pillar, she who loved fresh spring water to drink, and who spun her thread and wove her web in peace to guard that simple woman's home.

'From her dark abode within the crack in the doorpost, she felt the ground begin to tremble with the arrogant tramping of men. Peeping out she saw bold warriors hunting, and guessed that some trickery was soon to pass. Quick as the wind itself this wise weaver ran across the roof and took her secret way into the backwards room where the baby slept. She flexed her delicate legs and spun and spun and spun, working until the entire cradle was covered in a thick grey web. Just as she scuttled into the roof timbers to hide, the inner door was flung wide open.

"Any babies in here? Any babes new-born? They must be counted! We have come to take them to the place of counting!" And whether it was virtue in the web or whether it was that men have always been afraid of spiders, no one knows, but they looked at the place where the cradle stood and saw nothing.

"Ha! No babies here brother, she doesn't even *clean* this room!. Let's be gone!" And they stamped off shouting and rattling their clubs against their shields, as such men do. Of course the child in that cradle was a special child who did many wonderful deeds when she grew up, but those are in stories for other years to come. You may have guessed by now that one of her deeds, though it was a lesser one, was to carry that curse to the false king and destroy him and his line forever.

'So listen my children and remember. Three things that are never to be done: to kill the spider, to count the people, to wake the babe new-born.'

Her voice was dry as she leaned over to strike the gong beside the Horn Chair. In a chorus the children replied to the Woman of the Birds, looking up at her:

'We listen and remember, Mother of All.' And the solemn crowd dissolved into chattering children; the smallest of all, who were asleep, were carefully carried out into the sun by their brothers and sisters. As soon as the door to the Hall closed, whooping and shouting began, and the sound of games being played. Only one small girl remained. She bit her knuckles and bowed her head, then looked up at the tiny withered old woman upon the High Chair.

'Well daughter, what question must you ask me?' croaked the Woman of the Birds. The girl stood up, first upon one foot, then upon the other, not daring to speak. The sound of laughing and playing outside made her turn her head, drawing her back to the lovely day. Almost she ran off to join the others, but at last she pulled her fingers from her mouth and said...

'Mother of All, what happened to the horse?'

(Two further episodes of this title can be found in R.J. Stewart's *Magical Tales*, also published by The Aquarian Press.)

APPENDIX

YOUNG TAM LIN

1. The King forbad his maidens all
   That wore gold in their hair
   To come and go by Carterhaugh
   For the Young Tam Lin was there.

2. And those that go by Carterhaugh,
   From them he takes a fee,
   Either their rings or their mantles,
   Or else their maidenheads.

3. So Janet has kilted her green mantle
   Just a little above her knee,
   And she has gone to Carterhaugh,
   Just as fast as she could flee.

4. She had not pulled a double rose,
   A rose but three and four,
   When up and spoke the Young Tam Lin,
   Crying 'Lady, pull no more!'

5. 'How dare you pull those flowers,
   How dare you break those wands,
   How dare you come to Carterhaugh
   Withouten my command?'

6. (She said) 'Carterhaugh it is my own,
   My father gave it me,
   And I will come and go by here
   Withouten any leave of thee!'

7. There were four and twenty ladies gay
   A sitting down at chess,
   In and come the fair young Janet
   As pale as any glass.

8. Up and spoke her father dear,
   He spoke up meek and mild:
   'Oh alas, Janet' he cried
   'I fear you go with child.'

9. 'And if I go with child,
   Indeed it is myself to blame,
   There's not a lord in all your hall
   Shall give my child his name!'

10. So Janet has kilted her green mantle
    Just a little above her knee,
    And she has gone to Carterhaugh
    For to pull the scathing tree.

11. 'How dare you pull that flower
    All among the leaves so green,
    And all to kill the bonny babe
    That we got us between.'

12. 'Oh you must tell to me Tam Lin,
    Ah you must tell to me,
    Were you e'er a mortal knight
    Or mortal hall did see?'

13. 'I was once a mortal knight,
    I came hunting here one day,
    And I fell from off my horse,
    The Fairy Queen stole me away.'

14. 'Tomorrow night is Halloween
    And the fairy folk do ride,
    And those that would their true-love win
    At Miles Cross they must hide.'

15. 'First you let pass the black horse
    Then you let pass the brown,
    But run up to the milk-white steed
    And pull the rider down.'

16. 'I, Tam Lin, on a milk steed,
    With a gold star in my crown,
    Because I was a mortal knight
    They give me such renown.'

17. 'First they'll change me in your arms
    Into a lion wild,
    But hold me close and fear me not,
    As you would hold your child.

18. 'Next they'll change me in your arms
    Into some snake or adder,
    Hold me close and fear me not,
    For I'm your child's father

19. 'Then they'll change me in your arms
    Into some burning lead,
    Throw me into well water,
    And throw me in with speed.

20. 'Last they'll change me in your arms
    Into a naked knight,
    Wrap me up in your green mantle,
    And hide me close from sight.'

21. So well she did what he did say,
    She did her true love win,
    She wrapped him up in her mantle,
    As blithe as any bird in spring.

22. Up and spake the Fairy Queen,
    And angry cried she:
    'If I have known of this Tam Lin,
    That some lady'd borrow thee . . .'

23. Up and spake the Fairy Queen
    From out of a bush of broom
    Crying 'Hark, my sisters all,
    Young Tam Lin has escaped his doom.'

24. 'If I'd have known of this Tam Lin,
    That some lady'd borrow thee
    I'd have plucked out thine eyes of flesh
    And put in eyes from a tree . . .

25. 'If I'd have known of this, Tam Lin,
    Before we came from home,
    I'd have plucked out thine heart of flesh
    And put in a heart stone.'

NOTES AND REFERENCES

1. Stewart, R.J., *The UnderWorld Initiation*, Mercury Publishing, North Carolina, 1998.
2. Stewart, R.J., *Advanced Magical Arts*, Element Books, Shaftesbury, 1989.
3. Stewart, R.J., *The Merlin Tarot* (Book and full colour deck of cards, illustrated by Miranda Gray), Aquarian Press, Wellingborough, 1988.
4. Matthews, John and Stewart R.J., *Warriors of Arthur*, Blandford Press, London, 1987.
5. Stewart, R.J., *Cuchulainn*, Firebird Books, Poole, 1988.
6. Matthews, Caitlin, *Mabon and the Mysteries of Britain*, Arkana, London, 1987. Also Ashe, Geoffrey, 'Merlin in the Earliest Records' in *The Book of Merlin* (edited Stewart R.J.), Blandford Press, Poole, 1987.
7. Matthews, John, 'Merlin in Modern Literature' in *The Book of Merlin* (ibid).
8. Stewart, R.J., *Living Magical Arts*, Blandford Press, Poole, 1987.
9. Rees, Alwyn and Brinley, *Celtic Heritage*, Thames and Hudson, London, 1978.
10. Stewart, R.J., *The Mystic Life of Merlin* (translation and interpretation of the twelfth century *Vita Merlini* of Geoffrey of Monmouth), Arkana, London, 1986.
11. Pollack, Rachel, *The New Tarot*, Aquarian Press, Wellingborough, 1989. Also Shephard, John, *The Tarot Trumps, Cosmos in Miniature*, Aquarian Press, Wellingborough, 1985.
12. Macdonald, D.A., and Bruford, Alan, *Memory in Gaelic Story-Telling*, University of Edinburgh, Offprints from Scottish Studies, Vol 22:1978.
13. Stewart, R.J., *Where is Saint George?* (Imagery in English folk-

song), Blandford Press, London, 1989.

14. Yates, Frances A., *The Art of Memory*, Routledge and Kegan Paul, London, 1972.

15. Stewart, R.J., *Celtic Gods and Goddesses*, Blandford Press, London, 1989.

16. Stewart, R.J., 'The Grail as Bodily Vessel' in *At The Table of The Grail* (edited J. Matthews), Arkana, London, 1988.

17. Ross, Dr Anne, *Pagan Celtic Britain*, Cardinal, London, 1974.

18. Stewart R.J., and Matthews J., *Legendary Britain*, Blandford Press, London, 1989.

19. Stewart, R.J., *The Waters of The Gap* (Mythology of Aquae Sulis), Ashgrove Press, Bath, 1989.

20. Stewart, R.J., *The Prophetic Vision of Merlin* (translation and interpretation of the twelfth century *Prophecies of Merlin*), Arkana, London, 1986.

21. *The Birth of Merlin*, a play attributed to William Shakespeare and William Rowley (1622), a new edition with introductions by Denise Coffey, R.J. Stewart, Roy Hudd, Element Books, Shaftesbury, 1989.

22. Cassette tapes of *Magical Tales*, *Magical Songs*, and *Meditations* are available from Sulis Music, BCM 3721, London WC1N 3XX.